Stripping Away the Barriers to Your Success in Sales

Joe & Dawn Pici
with Guy Harris and Jean (JJ) Brun

Edited by:
Guy Harris and Shirley Voorhees

Cover Design, Layout and Graphics:
Pedro A. Gonzalez

Published by Personality Insights, Inc.
PO Box 28592 • Atlanta, GA 30358-0592
800.509.DISC • www.personalityinsights.com

ISBN 0-9773472-2-2

Printed in the United States of America
First Edition: January 2008
Second Edition: July 2008

*This book is dedicated to
Dr. Robert A. Rohm
and the Team at
Personality Insights
who have devoted their lives
to furthering the personal
awareness and development
of others.*

"How wonderful it is that nobody need wait a single moment before starting to improve the world."

- Anne Frank

"It's not about technique; it's about intent."

- *Joe Pici*

Table of Contents

Table of Contents

Foreword

I have been teaching and speaking on the applications of the DISC **Model of Human Behavior** full-time since 1992. I have attended, spoken at, or participated in hundreds and hundreds of training sessions and conventions around the world. I have seen and heard many speakers from all backgrounds and skill levels at these events. One time (and only one time) I offered to give my speaking time to another speaker. The speaker was Joe Pici.

On the day that I made this offer, Joe was speaking to a large group of business owners. As he spoke, he showed practical ways to use the DISC **Model of Human Behavior** in a sales environment. At one point I thought, "Wow, he is good! I think he knows how to apply this information to sales better than I do!" Joe and his wife, Dawn, really are that good.

Shortly after this event, Joe and Dawn came to Atlanta to participate in one of our Personality Insights certification training classes. We spoke and got to know each other better. During our conversations, Joe told me that he had developed a sales training program built on the DISC model. Since I had heard him speak, I knew that he had great insights and perspective. So, I offered to work with him to turn his concept into a book.

Joe is not a man to "play around." Within about a month, we had a draft of his manuscript in our office for review. I saw that it had great concepts in it and asked two of our master trainers, Guy Harris and Jean Brun, to work with Joe and Dawn on the project. As they worked together with the original manuscript, they found that the content was so rich that two books were needed to fully capture the value of Joe and Dawn's ideas. **Sell Naked On The Phone** represents the first half of that collaborative effort.

I am excited about what the concepts in this book will do for you when you apply them to your sales efforts. I am happy to have played a part in bringing this book from concept to reality. I know that you will gain major insights and perspectives to help you achieve higher levels of success. So, read, enjoy, apply, and succeed with me as we **Sell Naked On The Phone**.

God bless you!

Robert A. Rohm, Ph.D.

Founder and President

Personality Insights, Inc.

Atlanta, Georgia

Introduction

Do you want to...

- Book more meetings with new clients?
- Increase your closing rate?
- Boost your income?
- Create more new business with less windshield time?
- Grow your market share?
- Help new sales team members get up to speed?
- Improve customer retention?
- Decrease employee turnover?

If you answered "yes" to any of these questions, this book is for you.

Sell Naked On The Phone is part of the **Sell Naked Sales System**. This book is more than a simple collection of tips and techniques. It is part of a system. With a system, you can accomplish greater results in less time than you ever thought possible. Systems allow ordinary people to achieve extraordinary results.

What you hold in your hands is not based on theory. It is over seventy-five years of combined experience, perspective, and wisdom that you can draw from to become a highly successful sales professional. We built this system on solid experience in the application of basic principles of human behavior. From this experience we created a repeatable, principle-based, systems approach to sales that you can apply to quickly achieve success in sales.

Because we know your time is valuable, we have targeted, honed, and sharpened every thought in this book (and the one that follows it – **Sell Naked In Person**) to help you accomplish more as a sales professional. We promise to make every page count as you read about the system and how to make it work.

Sell Naked On The Phone will give you the skills, confidence, and tools to improve your ability to meet and connect with more new people. Specifically, we focus on using the phone as a tool in this process.

Why would we dedicate one whole book to using the phone as a sales tool? Because…

...many sales professionals actually fear the phone.

Since most people do not openly admit this fear, we have no reliable way to measure how many people are affected by it. In our experience, we have found that almost every sales professional admits some fear of the phone. In researching information for this book, we spoke with one psychologist who specializes in helping people to overcome their fears. He estimated that most, if not all, sales professionals experience at least mild to moderate fear of the phone. If this statement describes you, **Sell Naked On The Phone** will help you conquer this fear.

Dawn Pici, one of our master sales trainers, has this experience to share:

> Before I learned these principles and practices, I thought I was a pretty good sales professional. I knew I was better than average for my company, and my income was fairly consistent. I became extremely comfortable with my existing clients, many of whom I had inherited.
>
> This comfort with the status quo kept me at a good, but not great, level of success. I did not really know how to increase my sales. I struggled to expand existing client orders, and I really didn't enjoy looking for new business.

When I did pursue new leads, I failed more often than I succeeded. As a result, I often avoided the work of expanding my client base because it seemed like a waste of my time to keep pounding the pavement or making those dreaded cold phone calls. In many ways, I came to fear the phone.

This dread and frustration continued until I learned to apply the principles described in **Sell Naked On The Phone.**

Now, as I work with other sales professionals, I find that the majority of them are just like I was. They would rather service existing clients than contact prospective ones because of their frustration with, fear of, or lack of confidence in the telephone as a sales tool. I also find that once my clients expand and improve their skill with the telephone, their income level rises.

In the pursuit of greater profit, companies hire scores of talented sales professionals every year. These professionals have immense potential. But, if they don't conquer the fear and frustration attached to using the phone, they can, like me, settle into becoming mere *order takers* rather than stretching to become *order makers.*

You may be like many of Joe and Dawn's training clients. You might be either an individual sales professional or a sales manager working with an experienced team that has been in sales for years. You may have attended one of the finest business schools in the nation. Maybe you have gone to seminars to learn about products and services, effective presentation methods, and closing techniques. Yet still, you struggle to improve your results.

Using this starting point as the backdrop, we have identified three key issues that often hinder sales professionals in their pursuit of success.

Bogus Beliefs

Bogus Beliefs are preconceived ideas about sales that will limit your success. For example, we find that many people attempt to apply techniques and approaches that simply will not work for them. They attempt these techniques because they often do not truly understand themselves or their clients. Become a student of people – both of yourself and others. Learn about drives, motivations, communication styles, and decision-making approaches. Learn to understand people, and you will master yourself. Master yourself, and you will break the Bogus Beliefs that limit your success.

The Bullying Behemoth (the phone)

Though we advocate using the telephone as a time-saving and effort leveraging tool, we often encounter resistance from sales professionals on this point. Given the high number of sales professionals who admit that they fear the phone, this resistance should not come as a surprise . Many sales professionals view the telephone as a Bullying Behemoth – a giant, menacing device designed to hurt them – when they should see it as a Business Builder. We understand the fear, so we developed some tools to help you beat the Bullying Behemoth.

Broken Bonds (of trust)

People buy from people that they know, like, and trust. Once you overcome the Bogus Beliefs and the Bullying Behemoth, you have got to connect with a person.

Here's the challenge – you want to speak with decision

-makers and decision-makers are busy people. They often do not have time to talk. In addition, when you first contact them, they generally start from a position of low trust based on their past experiences with other sales people.

You know that you will give them better service than other sales people, but they do not yet know this fact. So, they enter the first conversation with you from a position of Broken Bonds of trust. Using the principles in **Sell Naked On The Phone**, you can bridge these Broken Bonds.

With Sell Naked On The Phone, you have a system that will strip away these barriers to success in sales.

We have seen companies increase revenue and gain market share while decreasing the cost of doing new business when they apply the principles on these pages. Dozens of letters in our files testify to the fact that sales professionals can double and triple their commissions with this system.

We wrote this book, based on the following Starting Expectations:

1. You plan to meet with your clients personally to present your product or service.
2. You have a general working knowledge of the **Model of Human Behavior** (we included a brief description in **Appendix 2** for your reference). We recommend that you read the companion resource, *You've Got Style*, as part of your study of this topic. (Purchase from www.personalityinsights.com or your local consultant.)

Now, let's get started so that you can learn to **Sell Naked On The Phone**...

About the Authors

Joe Pici

Master Sales Trainer, Sales Professional, Executive Coach, Certified Human Behavior Specialist

Achieving national success with his own marketing company as a top 25% producer, Joe coaches and trains on the complete sales cycle. Since 1992 he has helped sales professionals sharpen their skills for both creating appointments and closing sales.

Joe's background as a college level athletic coach, combined with his certification as a Human Behavior Specialist, lends to his direct, hard-hitting, results-oriented approach. Working with large international organizations, as well as small mom-and-pop sole proprietorships, he has equipped and empowered thousands of individuals to achieve outcomes well beyond their original expectations.

Dawn Pici

Master Sales Trainer, Sales Professional, Executive Coach, Certified Human Behavior Specialist

A business strategist specializing in the area of Interaction Dynamics, Dawn has developed programs that increase efficiency, encourage mutual respect and improve communication in teams, while reducing conflict in the workplace.

Through a twenty year career as a musician and educator, teaching all levels from kindergarten to college, she mastered the skills of communication and motivation. She then moved into sales and marketing to become a top volume producer.

Dawn and Joe currently reside in the Orlando, Florida area and have two children.

(www.piciandpici.com)

Guy Harris

Certified Human Behavior Specialist, Master Trainer on the Model of Human Behavior, Conflict Resolution Expert

Business owner, senior level business manager, and U.S. Navy submarine officer, Guy understands what it takes to work with people. He began his career as an engineer, so he often describes himself as a "recovering engineer." Now a trainer, speaker, and consultant, he has helped thousands of people across North America to communicate more effectively by understanding and applying the principles of human interaction.

Guy currently resides in the Indianapolis, Indiana area with his wife and two children.

(www.principledriven.com)

Jean (JJ) Brun

Certified Human Behavior Specialist, Master Trainer on the Model of Human Behavior, Behavior Symptoms Analysis Expert

Jean (JJ) Brun is a man who is purpose-driven. After 20 years with the Canadian military (15 within the Intelligence Branch) he founded JJ Communications, a training company dedicated to inform and enlighten people in the field of human behavior. Leaders and decision-makers around the globe turn to JJ to get them moving forward towards more effective communication practices.

JJ currently resides in Gatineau, Québec, with his wife and two children.

(www.jjcommunications.com)

1

Bogus Beliefs

Bogus Belief 1

Sales professionals get people to buy.

"A journey of a thousand miles begins with the first step."

- Chinese proverb

The biggest challenge in selling is... **selling.**

First, we need to clear up a common misperception. That misperception comes from how most people view and approach the profession of sales.

Most people enter the field of sales with little or no understanding of what really happens in the sales process. We find that many people view selling as "getting clients to buy products or services." This view creates two common approaches to sales training:

1. Developing great product knowledge, and
2. Learning a few key phrases to use at the right time to close the sale.

This is not our approach.

We agree that sales professionals need great product knowledge. We also agree that knowing what to say and when to say it can dramatically improve your sales results. While we agree on these two key points, we differ with the above definition of sales because the mindset behind it begins with a focus on the sales professional's need to get the deal.

Instead of focusing on getting the deal, we start from a completely different perspective.

We define selling this way:

> ***Selling is finding a way to help clients solve a problem or fill an unmet need.***

We have one corollary to this definition as well. If your product or service will not solve a problem or fill an unmet need for your client – disengage. Have integrity. Do not force the sale. Keep your focus on solving problems and filling needs, not on getting the deal.

"The real voyage of discovery consists not in exploring new landscapes but in having new eyes."

- *Epictetus (1st century A.D.)*

Better Belief 1 – Sales professionals offer people a solution to a problem or a way to fill an unmet need.

Bogus Belief 2

Great techniques and product knowledge will close sales.

This belief stems out of Bogus Belief #1 (sales professionals get people to buy). Because of Bogus Belief #1, much sales training and literature focuses on techniques to "get people to buy" instead of focusing on the people factors involved in the sales process.

We did not begin our approach to sales with the "offering people a solution to a problem" mindset. In fact, we started our efforts to sell products and services using the first definition of "getting the deal." We came to our current definition through much hard and painful experience.

Let's look at a story from Dawn's early sales experience:

I remember my first sales pitch. I was eleven years old, and our school had a magazine drive. To kick-off the drive, our teachers and the company representatives showed us all sorts of wonderful prizes for different levels of accomplishment. I remember coming home that first day with my order form and brochures. I was excited! I knew my product! I knew which prize I wanted! I knew my sales goal!

When I got home from school, I walked next door to ask for a sale. I was still excited... and nervous. I knocked. They answered the door. I did my pitch. They said "no." (Their child went to school with me, and they were not interested.) Hmmm...poor prospect.

I quickly realized that everyone in our town of eight houses had a child in the school except one. I quickly ran across the field to get to that home. I arrived just in time to see Kay (a friend from school) leaving with a big smile on her face and cash in hand. Hmmm...missed opportunity. (My first lesson in, "You snooze, you lose.")

Now I had to get my parents involved. I needed transportation to reach better territories. Fortunately for me, my dad had his own business which was open in the evenings. He said I could set up there and pitch to his customers. I remember thinking something along these lines, "Good location. Lots of traffic."

As I suspected, the business had lots of foot traffic, and many customers were willing to listen to my pitch. Unfortunately, most of them also had children

who went to my school. (Would I have to travel out of state to win this promotion?)

Things looked grim. I was becoming both discouraged and desperate. I tried new approaches. Without any formal sales training, I developed my own version of various popular closing techniques:

- The Puppy dog close – "Your kids need this magazine, Mister."
- The Ben Franklin close – "Let's take a look at all the good stuff you will get. I'll bet you don't have good stuff like this at home."
- The Order blank close – "How many magazines can I put you down for?"

I worked hard, but I had no success. I was about to give up when one of my dad's friends came into the shop. I knew three things about him:

- his kids were grown – they wouldn't be involved in the magazine drive;
- he lived far away – he probably had not been approached yet; and
- he was RICH – he had money available.

I began my pitch and then asked for the sale. Well, *ask* is not quite the right term. *Begged* would be a better word. Actually shameless, tearful begging would be the most accurate way to describe what got me my first sale.

Fast forward twenty five years. Before I entered corporate sales, I got my start in direct sales. At the beginning of this experience, I spent two months learning everything I could about my product line. I bought sample products. I learned fascinating product demonstration techniques.

When the time came for my first sales call, I

packed my bag, built a call list, and got ready to hit the road. I was now ready for what I considered the "fun part" – calling people and asking them to take a look at what I was selling.

First call: "My husband and I just got involved with a direct sales company and..." CLICK. My friend hung up on me! How rude! This treatment after I went to her jewelry party!

Next call: "Hi! Hey, I've got some great products that I want to show you. My husband and I just got involved with a direct sales company and ..." "No thanks." CLICK.

After an evening of calls that all went this way, I began to realize that being associated with a direct sales company was about as welcome as leprosy. What struck me as really odd about this situation was that everyone who tried the products from this company LOVED them. They just didn't want me to come over and SELL them.

Finally – discouraged, desperate, and in tears – I called my best friend. I begged her to at least let me show her what I had to sell. She agreed.

Once again shameless, tearful begging got me my first sale.

Dawn eventually became known nationally as one of the top 25% producers with that direct sales company (without tearful begging). She learned a lot along the way, and, in the process, Dawn found that success came when she learned to apply the definition we now use for selling. As a result, she and Joe have trained tens of thousands of people to become more effective sales professionals.

As we gained the experience that led to our current definition of sales, we learned another key concept:

Relationships form the foundation for all long-term, repeat sales.

Look at Dawn's story. She began her sales career working under the false impression that knowing her product or service and giving a great pitch would entice her clients to buy. She initially thought that either the products would sell themselves or that she could use a good closing technique to "get the deal."

"(If) selling were as simple as knowing your product… your function would be like a catalogue or reference book, supplying the correct answers to technical questions on demand. Once Mr. Prospect had all of the information, your job was finished. This, to be sure, is not how it is at all."

- James R. Fisher Jr.

Great products, flawless presentations and price comparisons may get you a few small sales. Memorizing some closing techniques will help you get a few more. However, to reap a large harvest in the sales profession, you have to step beyond depending upon the products to sell themselves or relying on memorized closing techniques.

You have to find ways that your product or service can help your customer, and you must effectively communicate this value to them. As you listen to your client and forge a good professional relationship, you will better understand their needs and desires. When you really understand their needs, you can better fill those needs.

We do recommend that you know your product and that you learn some closing techniques to use as appropriate. In fact, we will introduce some powerful techniques that we recommend in this book and in **Sell Naked In Person**. We just want to make the point here that techniques support your relationship, they do not replace it.

Without a good working relationship, techniques become skilled manipulation tactics for getting the sale rather than tools to help your customer reach a decision about solving their problem. When this happens, you increase the odds of creating customer dissatisfaction and buyer's remorse.

We will comment on this further when we discuss the concept of developing rapport with your client, but at this point let's look at one key concept that lies at the foundation of all relationships (business or personal). Relationships always begin with a personal connection, and personal connections always begin with communication between two people.

So, if the selling process begins with a personal connection and a personal connection begins with communication, then the selling process depends on clear, effective communication. Throughout our description of the **Sell Naked Sales System**, we will consistently focus on effective communication skills. Both telephone calls and face-to-face meetings depend heavily on good communication skills.

As you study the principles we present, remember that every communication has these six key components:

1. What you think you said
2. What you actually said
3. What the other person heard
4. What you think the other person heard
5. What the other person thinks about what you said
6. What you think the other person thinks about what you said

Our friend and colleague, Jean Brun, (also known as JJ) has a story to illustrate the significance of understanding this point:

> As a member of a multi-national military force serving in a foreign theater of operation, I quickly learned the value of clear and accurate communication. I also learned that the idea we mean to communicate, and what we thought we said, may not be what the other person heard, or understood, when we said it.
>
> This multi-national force had representatives from several countries, and we used "English" as the common working language. While in theory we all spoke the same language, we definitely experienced some communication challenges. Early in my tour of duty, I learned that my French-Canadian "English" differed significantly from the "English" spoken by the British, Spanish, German, Belgian, Dutch and American team members. As one of my commanders used to say:
>
> > "I know that you think you understand what I just said, but I'm not really sure that what you think is what I meant for you to understand... understand?"
>
> Operating in this hostile environment, I quickly learned to make no assumptions about what I actually communicated to people and, in turn, what they intended to communicate to me. As a result, I learned **the value of asking questions to verify and clarify the intended meaning rather than assuming that people understood me or that I understood them**. From this experience, I developed the following statement that I use in my Communicate with Insights workshops:
>
> **Communication is simple, it's just not easy!**

Becoming a great sales person calls you to become a great communicator. As you work with clients and prospective clients, remember JJ's point:

Communication is simple, it's just not easy!

By applying the **Sell Naked Sales System**, you can master the six components of great communication in order to become the communicator and sales person you desire to become.

Ultimately, your ability to communicate value to your clients and to find ways to solve their problems will come out of your connection with them and not from a closing technique.

"Personal relationships are the fertile soil from which all advancement, all success, all achievement in real life grows."

- Ben Stein

Better Belief 2 - A great connection with your client will close more sales.

Bogus Belief 3

One "magical" approach exists that works for all sales people with all clients.

Remember this point – people, not businesses, buy products and services. Every cash exchange, check payment, credit card transaction, and purchase order originates with a person making a decision to buy. This simple fact explains why we built the **Sell Naked Sales System** on the principles of human behavior and relationship dynamics. People make decisions to buy, and the decision to buy is the desired goal of every sales effort.

Because relationships drive sales, developing the ability to quickly and effectively build positive relationships lies behind sales success. The ability to understand people – their motivations, frustrations, wants, and needs – supports the process of building positive relationships. Since these drivers come from within a person, we cannot directly observe them. While we cannot see internal drivers, we can see external behaviors. From the study of human behavior, we know that external behaviors start with one of these internal drivers.

So, we can apply careful observation of behavior to develop an educated guess about the internal drivers. We use the DISC **Model of Human Behavior** as the tool to facilitate this understanding.

We assume that you have at least a working knowledge of the DISC **Model of Human Behavior**. We have included an appendix (Appendix 2) describing this model for you to use as a reference or as a starting point if you have not studied the model before. We strongly recommend that you also read one of Dr. Rohm's other books that describe the model in greater detail (*You've Got Style, Positive Personality Profiles, or Who Do You Think You Are… anyway?*).

While we don't propose that you attempt to use the model to over-read a person or delve into some type of deep psycho-analysis, we do recommend that you develop a good working knowledge of what tends to drive human behavior. With this working knowledge, you will have a better understanding of what you might do that sends unintended messages to your clients, what might motivate your client to move towards a buying decision, and how you can modify your behaviors (both words and actions) to improve the connection you make with your clients.

To illustrate this point, let's look at an experience Dr. Robert Rohm, our expert on this topic, had as a parent:

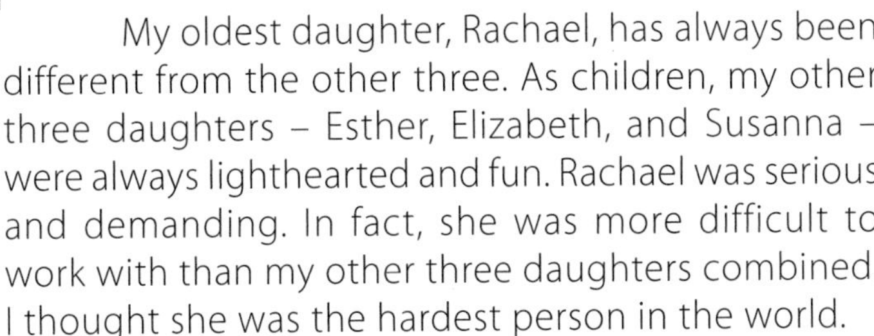

My oldest daughter, Rachael, has always been different from the other three. As children, my other three daughters – Esther, Elizabeth, and Susanna – were always lighthearted and fun. Rachael was serious and demanding. In fact, she was more difficult to work with than my other three daughters combined. I thought she was the hardest person in the world.

When Rachael was twelve, a friend of mine was passing through town, and he stopped to visit. As we were talking, I told him, "I'm very concerned with Rachael."

He said, "What's wrong?"

I said, "I don't know."

You see, I had a problem, but I did not know what the problem was. So, I did not know how to fix it. In fact, I did not even know where to begin.

That night my friend said, "Have you ever given her a personality profile assessment?"

I said, "What's that? I've never heard of that before."

He said, "It's an assessment where a person answers questions about their likes and dislikes. It gives you insight into how they see the world. Would it be alright if I gave her an assessment?" Well, I wanted to understand my daughter better so I said, "Sure."

He gave Rachael the assessment, and he scored it. Then he showed me the results. I had never seen anything like it before. He said "Wow, she is a very High-**D**."

I asked, "What does that mean?"

"You know: dominant, direct, demanding, dictatorial, decisive, and a doer." he explained.

With amazement, I said, "You are exactly right! How do you know that?"

He said, "That's how she scored on her profile. Tell me, do you have any trouble with her at bedtime?"

Again I was amazed at his insights. I said, "Yes, as a matter of fact, I do."

He said, "I am just curious about one thing. What do you tell her at bedtime?"

I said, "I tell her, 'Rachael, you need to be in bed by ten o'clock.'"

He looked at me with disbelief and said, "That's what you say to her?"

I said, "Yes. What is wrong with that?"

He said, "When you say that to a **D**, that may be what you say, but that's not what she hears. What she hears is. 'Do you want to fight?' "

I said, "How do you get, 'Do you want to fight?' from, 'You need to be in bed by ten o'clock.' "

He said, "You just don't understand **D**'s. They like control and choices. They like to be in charge. You see, you need to learn to say the same thing in a different way. When you say 'You need to be in bed by ten o'clock,' it sounds pushy and controlling to her so she doesn't respond well."

At that moment I thought, "This is both interesting and frustrating. I've known Rachael for twelve years. He has known her for twelve minutes, and he knows more about her than I do!"

The next night, I changed my approach with Rachael. I said, "Rachael, tonight you can go to bed

whenever you like. You have complete control. The limit is ten o'clock." As the words left my mouth, I thought, "This will never work."

To my amazement, she went into her room just before ten o'clock, closed the door and went to bed. I said the same thing in a different way, and she cooperated with me instead of fighting against me.

In this story, Dr. Rohm had to "sell" the idea of going to bed by ten o'clock to his daughter, Rachael. Before he understood her motivations, he experienced conflict, stress, and poor results. When he learned how to speak to her in a way that connected with her desires, he experienced great results. With one small shift in approach, he "sold" Rachael on the value of being in bed on time.

In the twenty plus years since this story, Dr. Rohm has become a world renowned expert on the topic. Like Dr. Rohm, you can also learn how to "read" behavioral traits. Once you develop this skill, you can know a person better in a matter of minutes than you would in months if you did not have this understanding.

With the **Sell Naked Sales System**, we have designed a step-by-step process that you can use to apply the **Model of Human Behavior** to the selling process. This system will take you from your current sales skills level (even if it involves tears) to confidence and enhanced achievement.

Successful application of the principles and practices in the **Sell Naked Sales System** begins with understanding your personality style. Not every approach works for every sales person. We have all read some great books on sales that promote approaches that only the author or someone like him (or her) could effectively apply. As a result, we recommend that you become a student of human behavior and that you make yourself your first object of study. Based on this self knowledge, you can then use the principles in this book to modify the techniques to fit you and your situation.

Most people can recognize the communication style differences between people – verbal (word choice), non-verbal (body language), and vocal (voice tones and inflection). The non-verbal and vocal clues often communicate much more than your words. As a result, using an approach that does not fit your personality style might create inconsistency between your words, your vocal tones, and your body language. Often, your client will sense, or feel, this inconsistency. If this happens, you run the risk of breaking your connection with them or, even worse, damaging their trust. We do not advocate hiding behind your personality style, we do suggest that you use your strengths to the greatest benefit as opposed to becoming someone that you are not.

Here is a story from Guy's experience to illustrate this point:

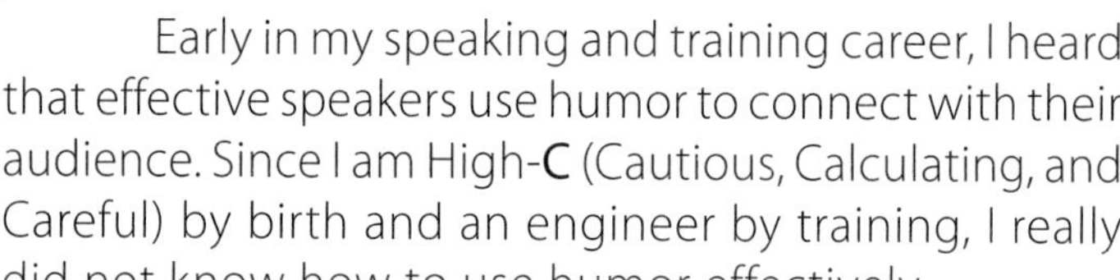

Early in my speaking and training career, I heard that effective speakers use humor to connect with their audience. Since I am High-**C** (Cautious, Calculating, and Careful) by birth and an engineer by training, I really did not know how to use humor effectively.

The only mental model I had for humor in speaking came from watching Dr. Rohm. When he speaks in front of an audience, his High-**I** (Inspiring, Interesting, and Impressive) nature shines and engages the audience. So, I tried to use humor like Dr. Rohm

does. Initially, I imitated his body language and vocal tones in my presentations. I soon realized that people thought he was funny when he behaved like he does and that they perceived me as goofy when I did the same things.

High-**I** behaviors coming from a High-**C** body just don't play well. No matter how hard I try, I don't look natural and relaxed when I "put on" someone else's style.

I quickly learned that I do not "do" Dr. Rohm's style very well, but I can "do" Guy's style with exellence. As a result, I had to learn how to imitate the thought behind what Dr. Rohm did rather than try to imitate the behavior. When I began to understand the principles of humor rather than try to memorize a technique, I found an approach that works for me.

Like Guy's presentation approach, sales approaches can come across the same way. An approach that seems relaxed, natural and concerned from one person might look stiff, forced and manipulative from someone else. We suggest that you learn both the principles and the practices of the **Sell Naked Sales System**. Further, we recommend that you focus on the thought, or principle, behind the practice more than you do on memorizing the words. The words can guide you as you get started, but don't let them limit your creativity.

Better Belief 3 – When you learn to control your personality style, you will connect with your clients better and you will close more sales.

2

Becoming Your Best Self

Becoming Your Best Self

Your search for extraordinary sales skills begins with you: your needs, your fears and your motivations. Every person on this planet *needs* to have their needs filled. As a sales professional, you are no different. Here is the insight Joe and Dawn have learned through years of helping sales people improve their closing rate:

- Your internal desire to have your needs met creates your behaviors.
- Your behaviors send messages to your clients.
- Your clients respond to all of the messages you send: verbal, vocal, and non-verbal.

Even if they only sense the messages subconsciously and cannot tell you what they pick up from you, their sense of what you are communicating still drives their behaviors. When your behaviors communicate that you are not genuine, or are working to meet your own needs, you repel potential clients. When they sense that you are working to meet their needs, they will tend to trust you more and to feel a closer connection (at least in a business sense) with you. The resulting trust and connection will lead to more sales.

When many trainers talk about meeting needs in the sales process, they usually refer to the client's needs and finding ways to meet them. We agree that sales depend on your ability to meet your client's needs. In addition, we have learned another critical point often overlooked in sales training programs.

Your ability to meet your client's needs hinges on your ability to make the most of your strengths and to minimize the negative impact of your blind spots.

By recognizing your own needs and drives and how they may either help or hinder your performance, you can make the behavioral adjustments necessary to really connect with your clients.

In the following chapters we will take a closer look at what "makes you tick" so that you can learn to recognize when these drives begin to push you towards uncontrolled, or out-of-control, behaviors. Out-of-control behaviors hurt your ability to connect with your clients.

"When you're in a hole, stop digging."

- Ian McIver

In-control vs. Out-of-control

Every personality style has unique strengths that make success in sales attainable. These strengths make every personality style a good one to have. Unfortunately, strengths can be pushed to an extreme and then become blind spots.

You may notice that we generally use the phrase "blind spot" rather than the word "weakness" in discussing personality styles. We have found that the word "weakness" may sound negative. It can imply that you cannot improve in that particular area. A blind spot is simply an area where you need some assistance to "see."

Here is how Guy describes the difference between a weakness and a blind spot:

> Consider a car that has a top design speed of 100 miles per hour. This car would be great for driving on Interstate highways at 70 miles per hour, but it would not be safe for driving in a NASCAR event

where qualifying speeds can be in the 150-190 mile per hour range. The top speed of this car would be a weakness that you could not overcome without significant redesign (new engine, new transmission, new suspension, etc.).

This same car, like every car, has certain areas around it where the driver cannot see without mirrors. These areas would be the driver's blind spots. For example, the driver cannot see out of the back window of the car while facing forward. Unlike the weakness, the car's top speed, you can fix the blind spot with a small design adjustment – add some mirrors. The mirrors do not remove the blind spot – the driver must still take action to see in that area – but the adjustment is minor compared to the changes necessary to overcome the car's weakness.

In our experience, people can hear or see the word "weakness" and then give up the hope that they can improve in that area. This observation comes from years of working with thousands of people as we teach these concepts. In fact, you may even see the word "weakness" used in Personality Insights materials published several years ago. Like you, we continue to learn and grow.

Just to make sure we are clear, we will restate the difference. You can compensate for a blind spot with minor adjustments. Weaknesses require significant "redesign."

For example, the High-**D** perspective is opposite the High-**S** perspective in the personality style circle.

A person with High-**D** traits will have no problem seeing situations from a **DOMINANT** perspective because that's how they naturally view nearly everything. However, they may struggle to see things from a **SUPPORTIVE** perspective. In other words, they tend to feel comfortable taking charge and uncomfortable in a helping role. This perspective is not inherently good or bad. However, it can be pushed to an extreme.

Under control, the High-**D** sales person often feels comfortable in negotiations and in closing the sale. Both of these parts of the sales process lead to results, and High-**D**'s are often driven by getting results. Out-of-control, the High-**D** sales person can become pushy or aggressive with clients in an attempt to close the sale and move on to the next one. They might feel uncomfortable slowing down and giving their client the time to reach a decision without pressure.

Joe has a great story to illustrate this point:

Once I went on a sales call with Bob, a High-**D**. Bob was calling on Frank, a High-**S**, to present a new

product line for Frank's consideration. Bob needed one more sale to qualify for a sales contest his company was running. The sales call happened on the last day of the month, and the qualifying period for the contest ended at the close of business that day.

During the presentation, Bob used controlled voice tones and a slower pace to connect well with Frank. He used great questions like, "How can I help you?" and, "What would make your life easier?" as he presented the new product line to Frank. While he was in control of the presentation, Bob did a great job of connecting with Frank.

After Bob finished his presentation, Frank sat back and thought for a moment. Then he said, "I'm not familiar with this type of product. Can you help me understand how it works?"

Bob leaned forward, raised his voice, and said, "Don't you understand how this product can be used for great results?"

Frank looked surprised at Bob's increased intensity, and he sat farther back from the table. He sat quietly for a moment. Then he said, "I am still unfamiliar with this product. I don't understand how this would work."

Bob, getting impatient with his client, said, "Trust me. This is what you are looking for." Frank said, "I like what you have. I just need some time to think this over. Can you give me some time?" Bob was now visibly agitated. He said, "How much time do you need? Can we close this today?"

Frank was not ready to close the deal that day or, for that matter, any other day. He no longer had any interest in doing business with Bob. Frank agreed to another meeting with Bob, but he cancelled it the

next day. Bob never met with Frank again.

I do not know everything that Bob was thinking during this discussion, but he appeared to shift from a supportive, helpful attitude to a dominant, controlling one in a flash. He seemed to be responding to his desire to close the sale by 4:00 p.m. rather than to his client's questions and concerns. Frank definitely requested help in a High-**S** fashion. He basically asked, "HOW does this work?" Bob responded with High-**D** intensity and language. He said, "This is WHAT you can accomplish!" In the pressure of the moment, he forgot about his client, and he pushed for results.

When Bob had control of the situation – while he was talking – he exhibited great personal control. As soon as control shifted to Frank, Bob began to feel the time pressure of closing the sale, so he reverted to his natural behaviors. Unfortunately, he not only broke the connection, he went so far as to actually irritate his client. He let his natural response move to an out-of-control mode, and he lost the sale. Because he irritated Frank, he even went farther than that. He lost the opportunity for any future sales as well.

We call extreme reactions, like the one Bob had, out-of-control behaviors. When we use the phrase out-of-control, we mean that a behavior comes from a natural, or subconscious, response, rather than from a controlled, or conscious, one. Out-of-control behaviors tend to happen when a situation triggers fears or frustrations. Each personality style carries with it a set of fears and frustrations. When triggered, these fears and frustrations create stress and pressure that can manifest in negative reactions.

In reference to out-of-control behaviors, notice that we use the word *reactions* and not *responses*. Understanding the difference between these two words will facilitate your understanding of how to become your *best self*. For our purposes, *reactions* are words or actions that come automatically. They happen without consciously thinking about them. *Reactions* come from your most natural way of acting, and they generally show up when you are under pressure. *Responses*, on the other hand, are words or actions that you reflect upon *before* you choose to act.

You can see the difference between these words by looking at how pin ball machines behave. The silver ball *reacts* to the pressure placed upon it by the flippers. As a result, it bounces between objects on the game board and goes wherever they direct it. The flippers are under the control of a person who is intentionally *responding* to the movements of the ball to direct it towards objects with the highest scoring value.

Your best self is you under control. When you are your best self, you use wisdom and discernment to choose the most appropriate words and behaviors for a given situation. You act to protect the interests of all parties concerned. In life, you can become your best self by choosing a response to produce the greatest value in any situation.

"Anger is a way of saying, 'Notice my needs'. That's why it is expressed when a person feels ignored, put down, or unappreciated by another person (or persons)."

- Les Carter, Getting the Best of Your Anger

3

General Insights for Every Sales Professional

General Insights for Every Sales Professional

As you read the following section, notice that we based it on the brief description of the four basic personality style traits contained in Appendix 2.

Remember: You are a blend of all four personality styles.

You will probably identify best with the traits in one of the type descriptions. Because you are a blend of all four styles, you may also see parts of your personality style in one or two of the other type descriptions. You are likely to identify least with the remaining type descriptions. This is perfectly normal.

We suggest that you initially focus your attention on developing a growth plan based on your primary personality style. As you learn to use the strengths and compensate for the blind spots in your primary style, you can then focus your attention on other aspects of your unique style blend.

It is possible to form a fairly accurate picture of your basic personality style blend by simply reading the following sections and looking for statements and perspectives that fit your natural perspective. For a more complete picture of your unique style blend, we recommend that you complete a personality profile assessment.

With the results of a personality profile assessment in-hand, you can work with a mentor skilled in applying this information to gain the greatest benefit from this study. If you do not have a mentor skilled in applying this information, we recommend that you get a custom-prepared DISCovery Report. This report will identify, with great accuracy, how your blend operates in life and in business. It will reveal your natural strengths and also highlight the struggles you may face in adapting your style. The report includes specific suggestions for creating an action plan to help you achieve greater success. The DISCovery Report is useful in working with a mentor, but it becomes even more valuable if you do not have this person in your life.

> You can order your DISCovery Report by contacting the person who supplied you with this book or at the Personality Insights website (www.personalityinsights.com).

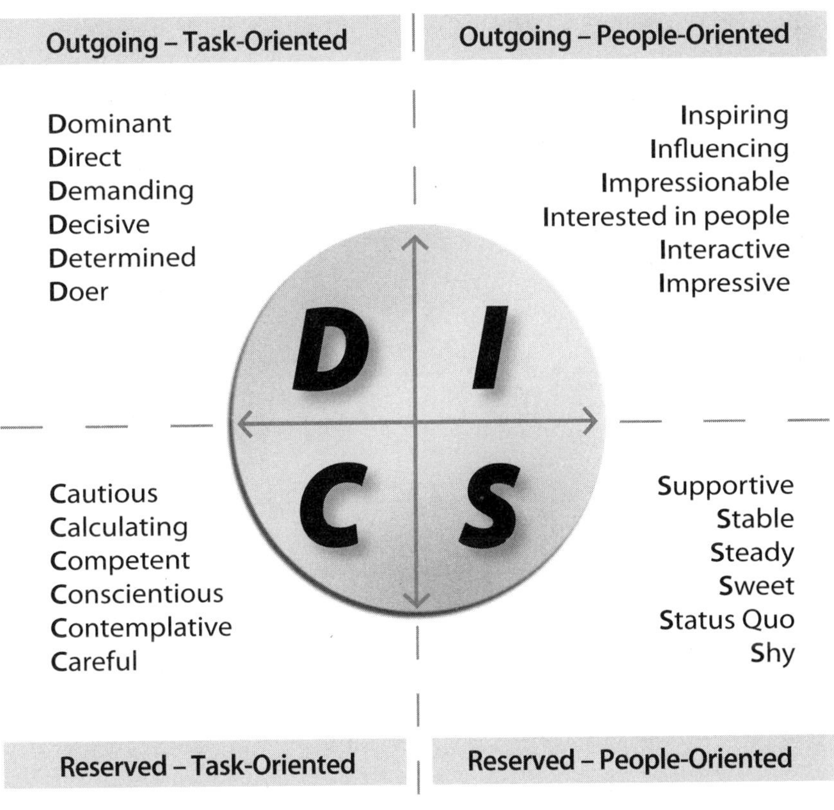

THE HIGH-D SALES PROFESSIONAL

As a two year old this person's first sentence was probably "I do it MYSELF!" They continue to say that for the rest of their lives. People with High-**D** traits approach everything they do with energy, focus, and tenacity.

Key quote for the High-**D** sales professional:

"Mental toughness is many things and rather difficult to explain. Its qualities are sacrifice and self-denial. Also most importantly, it is combined with the perfectly disciplined will that refuses to give in. It's a state of mind – you could call it character in action."

- *Vince Lombardi*

Can be described as:	Dominant, Direct, Demanding, Decisive, Determined, Doer
Characterizing Symbol:	Exclamation point – You are emphatic in everything! !
Characterizing Color:	Green – for go
Outlook on life:	You probably like to lead or be in charge.
Focus:	Get the job done – just do it! Overcome opposition and achieve your goals! Winners never quit and quitters never win!
Ideal environment:	Upbeat, fast, powerful

People with High-D traits make great sales professionals because they:

- Set clear sales goals and persist to accomplish them
- Do not get disturbed by the word NO. To them, NO means ASK AGAIN LATER
- See opportunities, not problems
- Like competition and respond positively to sales promotions
- Have tremendous energy
- Have the drive to achieve Top Producer status
- Have innovative ideas
- Enjoy the independence of a sales position
- Make decisions quickly and then work to make the decisions happen
- Like negotiating
- Will work long hours
- Like to solve problems

HOW TO BE THE BEST HIGH-D POSSIBLE

The High-**D** personality is great for sales! If this is you, you have the drive, the focus, and the persistence to accomplish any task or challenge. In fact, you may view conquering challenges as fun. It can drive you to succeed. Your need to have a challenge is a huge asset.

High-D's NEED:

- Challenges
- Control
- Choices

These three needs make sales attractive to people with High-**D** traits. People with High-**D** traits often want to be their own boss. They want to have the control to make decisions and to have choices so that they control their destiny. They are generally self-motivated and task-oriented so they enjoy being the lone wolf while running the roads. They tend to view every potential sale as a challenge to meet with determination. They are often comfortable using a direct, matter-of-fact approach. They usually exhibit great energy, and they value productivity.

"I did it MY way..."
- *Frank Sinatra from the song My Way*

Issues that often cause stress for High-D's:

- Being taken advantage of
- Losing control
- Being disrespected
- A slow pace
- Talk that does not lead to action

Under pressure High-D's may react with (Out-of-control):

- Impatience
- Sarcasm
- Pushing for results (forcing a close)
- Intense physical expression
- Loud vocal tones

People with High-D traits will get better RESULTS when they:

- Become accountable to someone or allow a mentor to critique their performance
- Slow down, cultivate active listening skills, and learn to speak in softer voice tones so that they avoid coming across as pushy or overbearing
- Remember to smile and take the time to socialize with the customer

---

"Everyone wants to be appreciated, so if you appreciate someone, don't keep it a secret."

- Mary Kay Ash

THE HIGH-I SALES PROFESSIONAL

The theme song for High-I's could be "Don't worry, be happy." They love to have fun and to interact with other people.

Key quote for the High-I sales professional:

> "It almost doesn't matter what product I sell, customers enjoy buying from me!"
>
> *- Bill Porter*

Can be described as:	Inspiring, Influencing, Impressionable, Interactive, Impressive, Involved
Characterizing symbol:	Star – Give them a RED STAR! They need to be noticed and recognized. ★
Characterizing color:	Red – it says "Notice me!"
Outlook on life:	They like to persuade others to their way of thinking.
Focus:	I am for you! Let's have some fun! If we all pull in the same direction, our success will never end!
Ideal environment:	Fun, friendly, exciting

People with High-I traits make great sales professionals because they:

- Like to meet new people. They make cold calls warm within a few moments
- Project a likable attitude
- Enjoy interacting with people, they speak to others with ease

- Show enthusiasm
- Inspire customers to buy
- Have tremendous energy
- Will work hard because they want to please and impress superiors
- Work well in an informal or unstructured environment
- Quickly adapt to changes, they have great flexibility
- Add fun and excitement to the work place
- Encourage others
- Exude optimism

HOW TO BE THE BEST HIGH-I POSSIBLE

The High-I personality is great for sales! If this is you, you likely live to inspire and influence anyone who gets within five feet of you. You probably love people and feel comfortable speaking with almost anyone.

High-I's NEED:

- Recognition
- Approval
- Popularity

Gaining the acceptance, love, and admiration of the multitudes (the more the merrier) fuels many people with High-I traits. They often enjoy the limelight that sales presentations place upon them. They not only want to make the sale, they usually want the client to love them. They often mix their sales pitches with many humorous anecdotes. In their effort to keep the spotlight on themselves, they might dominate the conversation. At times, they can talk the ears off of a corn stalk! Very little stimulates them more than public recognition for their sales accomplishments.

Their driving need for popularity and social acceptance might create an equally strong fear of social rejection. In the face of rejection, High-I's tend to react emotionally.

> "Humor is by far the most significant activity of the human brain."
>
> - *Edward de Bono*
>
> *Leading authority in the field of creative thinking*

Issues that often cause stress for High-I's:

- Rejection
- Public embarrassment
- Loss of social standing and recognition
- Large quantities of detailed information
- Highly structured environments

Under pressure High-I's may react with (Out-of-control):

- Talking
- Laughing
- Emotion
- Diverting attention
- Joking

People with High-I traits will have more FUN when they:

- Get organized and avoid misplacing orders and contact information
- Focus on their goals and the task at hand to become a great finisher

- End their day on a positive note, listen to a motivational CD or read from a positive book. Avoid allowing one unsuccessful call or frustrating day to ruin their emotional outlook and productivity.

"No horse gets anywhere until it is harnessed...No life ever grows great until it is focused, dedicated, disciplined."

- Harry Emerson Fosdick

THE HIGH-S SALES PROFESSIONAL

People with High-**S** traits tend to have a quiet, laid back exterior. They generally like to work at a steady pace, and they usually like to know how things will turn out before they begin.

Key quote for the High-**S** sales professional:

"Take the trouble to stop and think of the other person's feelings, his viewpoints, his desires and needs. Think more of what the other fellow wants, and how he must feel."

- Maxwell Maltz

Can be described as:	Supportive, Stable, Steady, Sweet(nice/kind), Status quo, Shy
Characterizing Symbol:	Plus or minus sign – Either way is okay with them… They feel that harmony is what we need. $\pm$
Characterizing Color:	Blue – calm and serene like the clear, blue sky
Outlook on life:	They like to provide support to help complete the job.
Focus:	All for one and one for all! If we all work together we make a great team. All of us are better than one of us.
Ideal environment:	Predictable, stable, harmonious

People with High-S traits make great sales professionals because they:

- Listen well
- Make people feel comfortable and at ease
- Build strong relationships with their customers
- Create trusting relationships so that customers re-order
- Follow leadership well
- Finish what they start, once they get moving
- Avoid conflict and will keep the work place peaceful
- Like to work in a team environment; often willing to assist other sales people
- They give great customer service because they aim to please
- Have an easy-going approach
- Are dependable
- Feel comfortable doing repetitive tasks – follow through, etc.

HOW TO BE THE BEST HIGH-**S** POSSIBLE

The High-**S** personality is great for sales! If this is you, your ability to persist and finish what you start makes you the follow up and follow-through expert. You almost certainly excel at maintaining existing clients because you make time to get to know them, support their needs, and follow-through on your promises.

High-S's NEED:

- Appreciation
- Security
- Assurance

Little pleases people with High-**S** traits more than bonding with the people around them to accomplish a common goal. Warm-hearted, pleasant, and natural TEAM players, they often work behind the scenes to make things happen. When a problem occurs with a back-order or missed delivery, High-**S** sales people generally find a way to take care of the customer. They often do this personally. They might try to keep the peace regardless of the personal cost to them.

"Things come to those who wait, but only the things left by those who hustle."

- Abraham Lincoln

Issues that often cause stress for High-S's:

- Conflict
- Confrontation
- Loss of security
- Sudden change
- Multiple high-priorities with short deadlines

Under pressure High-S's can react with (Out-of-control):

- Procrastination
- Indecision
- Compromise
- Silence
- Withdrawal

People with High-S traits will get more COOPERATION when they:

- Project confidence in their product, service, or company
- Practice assertive communication skills to manage customer expectations – clearly define delivery dates, fees for extra services, etc.
- Recognize that a direct question or a "no" from a customer is not a personal attack.

"The best men are not those who have waited for chances but who have taken them; besieged the chance; conquered the chance; and made chance the servitor."

- E.H. Chapin

THE HIGH-C SALES PROFESSIONAL

People with High-**C** traits can achieve success in sales because of their relentless and methodical approach. They usually like to "plan their work and work their plan."

Key quote for the High-**C** sales professional:

"Reduce your plan to writing... The moment you complete this, you will have definitely given concrete form to the intangible desire."

- *Napoleon Hill*

Can be described as:	Cautious, Calculating, Competent, Conscientious, Contemplative, Careful
Characterizing Symbol:	Question mark – They want to know the "why" behind everything. ?
Characterizing Color:	Yellow – it stands for Caution
Outlook on life:	They like consistent quality and excellence.
Focus:	Anything worth doing is worth doing correctly. They want to provide quality goods and services through careful and conscientious work.
Ideal environment:	Structured, accurate, high quality

People with High-C traits make great sales professionals because they:

- Know their product(s) and service(s)
- Make clear and logical presentations
- Often anticipate and rehearse answers to the most likely questions their clients might ask
- Have very high standards for themselves
- Act with great integrity and honesty
- Finish whatever they start
- Seek perfection personally and professionally
- Carefully plan their work and work their plan. They will not entertain distractions
- Methodically work their territory
- Maintain objectivity
- Often analyze and pursue the most efficient approach to time and territory management
- Value loyalty

HOW TO BE THE BEST HIGH-C POSSIBLE

The High-**C** personality is great for sales! If this is you, you set high standards for yourself, and you are likely to study all of the details about whatever product or service you sell. Your methodical approach to handling your territory and your detailed preparation for every sales presentation makes you a valuable asset to your sales team. You probably strive for excellence and perfection in everything you do.

High-C's NEED:

- Quality answers
- Value
- Excellence

As highly logical thinkers, people with High-**C** traits carefully evaluate and explore all options to develop a procedure or plan to anticipate and prevent mistakes. They generally prepare well for every presentation. They may even speak from typed notes while referring to accurate graphs and research. They work hard to "keep all of their ducks in a row." They excel at organizing information, developing flow charts, and following rules.

"Integrity is the glue that holds our way of life together."

- *Billy Graham*

Issues that often cause stress for High-C's:

- Unknown or unclear expectations
- Illogical actions
- Disorganization
- Inconsistency
- Violating principles

Under pressure High-C's may react with (Out-of-control):

- Criticism
- Pessimism
- Asking pointed questions
- Judgment
- Correcting others

People with High-C traits will achieve EXCELLENCE when they:

- Recognize that "good enough" really is good enough so that they take action rather than over analyzing a situation.
- Learn how to give a brief overview of the presentation. Giving too many facts and details can make a sales presentation difficult to follow for other personality styles.
- Loosen-up and smile. Remember – people don't care how much you know until they know how much you care. A smile will create a better connection with more people.

"Look at failure from the perspective of gaining new insights. See failure for what it is – a data collection bank. With every failure, you gain new data, a deposit to draw upon for future success."

- *Gary Blair*

4

Working with People

Working with People

Once you have replaced your Bogus Beliefs about sales with Better Beliefs and start working to control your response to situations, you have begun the process of growing towards success in sales. You can now begin the process of learning to understand and work with other people so that you can more effectively help them solve their problems. Just as we teach the **Model of Human Behavior** as a tool for learning to control your behaviors, we also recommend that you use it as the primary tool in your effort to work with and understand other people.

Once you fully understand your personality style, both your strengths and your blind spots, you can move to better understand another person – your client. These two steps – first understanding yourself and then understanding your client – form the foundation for the **Sell Naked Sales System**.

Let's turn to our sales experts, Joe and Dawn Pici, to learn from their experience:

We believe in good sales technique, and we will get to that point later. For now, we want to emphasize the two critical people issues in the **Sell Naked Sales System** - understanding your own needs, drives and fears; and understanding your clients needs, drives, and fears. If you skip over this foundational information, you will miss the key principles that make the **Sell Naked Sales System** different from other training approaches.

In our discussions with Sales managers, they often tell us that they see a performance jump

shortly after a training program and then a decline back to pre-training levels after about 60-90 days. We often hear them say that they believe the drop in performance after the training honeymoon comes from poor motivation in their sales force.

This perspective does not fit our experience in working with sales people across the country. We find that most sales professionals are highly motivated. They want to apply what they have learned. They want to sell. They want to make money. They want to achieve success.

The problem lies, not with the sales people themselves, but with the structure of many sales training and motivational programs. These programs do not generally address the gap between the acquisition of knowledge and the application of knowledge.

Once the initial energy and enthusiasm of the training environment dissipates, they find that they have learned some new tips and techniques that may or may not fit their specific situation. Since many training programs teach techniques, but not foundational principles, these motivated and energetic sales professionals may find that they do not have the foundational knowledge to make adjustments to the techniques to fit them and their clients. So, they lose their enthusiasm and go back to their old way of doing things.

We find that this gap between knowledge acquisition and practical application often has more to do with lack of understanding of the needs and fears that drive behaviors than it does with motivation and knowledge. In other words, sales people are generally motivated and they usually know many great techniques. What they may not know is how

to effectively adjust those techniques to fit their own personality style and to match different types of clients. We also find that many otherwise fantastic sales professionals do not know how to overcome their own personal fears and performance-limiting thinking.

Most sales training programs focus on prospecting, contacting, product knowledge, presentation skills, handling objections and closing the sale. We agree that mastering these skills will lead to some success in sales. We have also found that these skills alone will not make you a long-term, mega-bucks sales success. In our work with sales professionals across the country, we have identified three additional, foundational skills that combine with the other sales skills mentioned above to produce an unbeatable combination. The three additional foundational sales skills are:

1. Control over your personal fears and drives
2. The ability to recognize your client's personality style. This knowledge includes:
    a. Recognizing their basic needs and fears
    b. Understanding how they may view you
3. Knowing how to adapt your behaviors and language to better connect with others.

We view these three items as skills and not as talents. A talent comes naturally to you. Talents cannot be learned. You learn skills when you have the right information, mentoring, and practice. We find that most people have natural strengths in some areas, and they struggle somewhat in others. Since these are skills

and not talents, anyone can overcome their personal struggles to master them. Anyone can learn these skills with the right information, the right coaching, and the right commitment to improve.

Notice that none of the foundational skills that Joe and Dawn list have anything to do with product knowledge. Nor do they refer to a one-size-fits-all method or technique for handling objections or closing the sale. These skills relate primarily to the ability to connect with the client – to build a good working relationship with them. This ability to connect with others comes from who you are as a person and not from a canned technique.

Consider master sales trainer, Zig Ziglar. He teaches people to handle objections, to make good presentations, and to close the sale. He also has a great number of seminars and resource materials targeted at developing personal excellence. Zig teaches skills, and he also says, "You've got to *be* before you can *do*. You've got to *do* before you can *have*." In other words, you have got to ***become*** a great sales person before you can experience sales success.

A successful sales professional must have exceptional product knowledge and an effective method for handling objections. They must also know how to close the sale. Unfortunately, too many sales people depend on these surface level skills and fail to grow in the foundational ones. The three elements that Joe and Dawn mention are critical to make the most of your presentation skills. Notice that each of the foundational skills relates to people skills and not to technical skills.

"There are two kinds of knowledge. One is general, the other is specialized. General knowledge…is of but little use in the accumulation of money."

- *Napoleon Hill*

Understanding the **Model of Human Behavior** is general knowledge. Understanding how it applies to you and your clients is specialized knowledge. General knowledge is nice to have. Specialized knowledge will lead you to success.

The specialized knowledge we teach is based on the definition of sales we used in the opening chapter of this book.

Selling is finding a way to help clients solve a problem or fill an unmet need.

With this as the starting point, we see all of the following techniques as tools in your sales toolkit to assist you in your effort to help your clients. Without the true desire to fill your client's needs, these approaches can look false and manipulative from your client's perspective. With the desire to help your client reach a quality decision, these approaches will increase your effectiveness.

We wrote everything that follows with the intent to help you develop the three foundational skills and to grow in specialized knowledge. Once you develop these skills, your booking rate will skyrocket!

5

Embrace the Phone

Embrace the Phone

"Joe and Dawn, because of you I'M GOOD!"

- Kathy, Orlando, FL

"Joe, your approach to the phone has been a tremendous success to our team. I have invested heavily in sales training over the past 30 years yet never received the results that your system produced. The way you approached it and got 100% buy-in was the best I've seen. An unbelievable approach!"

- Dutch Owens, Orlando, FL

Up to this point, we have introduced the background information that supports the **Sell Naked Sales System** and provides the foundation to assist you in your pursuit of sales success. Now, we move to the practical application steps you can follow to improve your effectiveness on the phone.

In writing this book, we assume that you are a sales professional or a sales manager involved in a business that requires direct, face-to-face contact at some point in the sales process. While the principles will apply to telemarketing or call center environments, the techniques and approaches we cover are primarily targeted at eventual face-to-face conversations.

Assuming that you want to see your clients personally, you must get an appointment before you can make the sales presentation or close the sale. Your business might use email marketing, newspaper and radio advertisements, direct mail, or some other form of marketing effort to generate sales leads.

These marketing efforts can create incoming calls for information or appointments, but the vast majority of sales for the person we thought about in developing this book (hopefully that's you) will start with the sales person contacting a potential client to schedule the appointment. The best tool for this type of contact is...the telephone.

In a seminar environment, we generally see two types of reactions as we move from background information to application tips and we mention actually picking up the phone. The two most common reactions are:

1. "Great, they're finally going to get to some practical stuff!"

   and

2. "Oh no. Now we have to pick up the phone!"

If you relate well to the first statement, you probably feel excited about getting down to business. If you relate more to the second statement, stick with us. We will show you some simple ways to overcome the pain, fear, or frustration you feel about making phone calls.

Let's get Joe's perspective on using the phone:

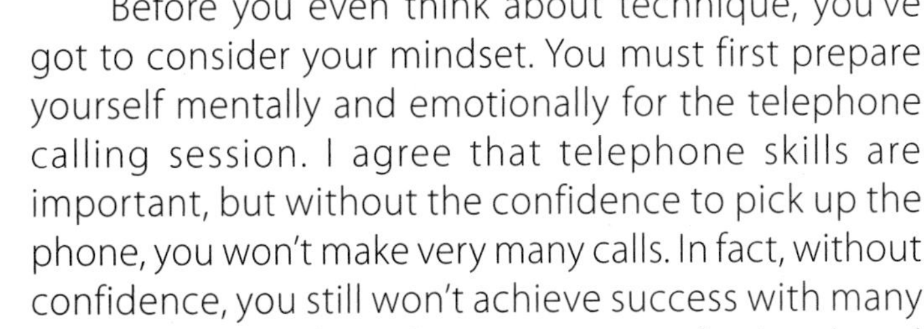

Before you even think about technique, you've got to consider your mindset. You must first prepare yourself mentally and emotionally for the telephone calling session. I agree that telephone skills are important, but without the confidence to pick up the phone, you won't make very many calls. In fact, without confidence, you still won't achieve success with many of the calls you do make. You are a professional, and you probably know that more phone calls lead to more

sales. If you are like most of the sales professionals that we have assisted, you know this fact and you still avoid making phone calls. However, to achieve real success in sales you must be aware of, confront, and overcome any fear, apprehension, or skepticism you have about using the phone.

The strength of the **Sell Naked Sales System** lies both in using the **Model of Human Behavior** to understand people AND in the approaches we have developed based on this understanding. By this point, you should have either taken a personality profile assessment or developed a pretty good idea of your basic personality style blend through the first part of this book. Speaking from a focused, driven, results-oriented, High-**D** salesperson's perspective, let me strongly encourage you to complete an assessment so that you have a full and accurate mental picture of your style.

Many of our clients initially resist investing the money or time to take an assessment. In fact, many of our clients insist that they already know their style and they don't need an assessment. I understand this perspective because I thought the same thing when I first learned about this material. However, after learning from Dr. Rohm and his staff, I now encourage everyone to take an assessment so that they really know their personality style blend.

When I began to better understand my own drives and behaviors, I started to find ways to more effectively apply my strengths and to overcome my blind spots. The system that Dawn and I have developed depends on a good working knowledge of the **Model of Human Behavior** – knowing where you fit within the model and understanding how to adjust yourself to different clients and situations.

Making yourself pick up the phone is one of the situations where you must bring your drives under control.

The success of these phone techniques depends on you accepting the idea that having the discipline and focus to use the telephone is your key to sales success. I stress this point because, as I conduct sales training, I hear just about every excuse you can name for not using the phone.

High-**D**'s often tell me that they don't have time to do the preparation I recommend for making phone calls. They often initially see my suggestions as "fluff." Let me assure you – they work.

High-**I**'s often tell me that they can book more appointments by driving around their territory and calling on people personally. They tend to see my suggestions as too rigid. Let me assure you – you will have more fun and receive more recognition if you will focus with me for a short time.

High-**S**'s seldom give direct objections to my methods, but they can be resistant because they don't want to bother anyone or seem too pushy. Let me assure you – my approaches help to create safe sales environments so that people want to work with you.

High-**C**'s usually object because they don't see the logic or value in my approach. Their initial hesitancy to pick up the phone usually comes from a desire to carefully analyze my suggestions. Let me assure you – I have carefully thought through every step of the process.

When I was a college football coach, I learned that every athlete has something that motivates them. I also learned that different people have different motivators. At the time, I didn't know how to quickly and easily identify each person's motivator. I really wish that I had known about the **Model of Human Behavior** then! Now I understand the common motivators for each personality style.

In the years since I moved from coaching to professional sales, here's what I have learned. If you can reframe the fear, apprehension, or skepticism that keeps you from making more phone calls, you will probably find the motivator to help you achieve success. As a football coach, I found that encouragement works better than pressure. It doesn't matter if I try to push you or if you apply the pressure yourself. You get the same result either way – resistance. So, here is my encouragement to you; identify the thing that stops you from making more calls, then reframe it to motivate and encourage yourself.

Every person has their own concerns and objections to different parts of this process. In fact, I had my own in the beginning of my sales career. For example, I will be suggesting that you develop a script to help you get started. As a High-**D**, I used to think the same thing many other High-**D**'s think about writing a script – it seemed like a waste of time. Then I reframed that thinking to tell myself that writing a script would tell me WHAT to do to achieve RESULTS from my phone calls.

Instead of letting my desire to immediately get to work drive me – making calls and "shooting from the hip" – I used my natural motivators to get me to do what I didn't really want to do in the beginning – write a script. As I have gotten more comfortable

with my script, I can now modify it on-the-fly. But, slowing down to write it in the beginning helped me get results faster.

In my experience, you can make more contacts and achieve more success in a well-planned 20 to 30 minute phone call session than you can by driving around your territory for two weeks. When you learn to use the telephone well, you will:

- Make more appointments
- Meet with better qualified clients
- Have fewer cancellations and no-shows
- Have more time to have fun
- Be better prepared to meet with clients because you will have a better indication of their personality style, and
- Net a higher percentage of sales.

From what Joe has experienced, developing telephone skills has something for everyone:

- Results for High-**D**'s
- Recognition and fun for High-**I**'s
- A comfortable pattern for High-**S**'s, and
- A predictable process for High-**C**'s

We see the telephone as a powerful tool in your sales toolkit. A tool that when used properly, can lead you to overwhelming success as a sales professional. So, we encourage you to...

...Embrace the Phone

6

Use the CALL Method

Use the CALL Method

Each individual telephone call will probably only last from 30 seconds to 2 minutes. So, you will have minimal time to accomplish your primary objective – booking a meeting! Since you will normally have such a short time on the phone, we have found that a simple, repeatable approach to placing your calls can significantly improve your results.

We have developed an acronym to help you remember the key components of an effective telephone call. We suggest that you use the **CALL** method where **CALL** stands for:

C CONNECT with the person on the phone

People will meet with you IF they like you or believe that you can help them solve a problem. Begin the phone call by connecting with your client. Learn skills to help you achieve a connection quickly.

A ANSWER the unspoken question, "Why are you calling me?"

Every person you call wants to know the answer to the question: "Why are you calling me?" Plan a good answer to this question and give it to them before they ask.

L LISTEN to their response

Learn to identify key information about your client simply by the way they respond to your introduction on the phone.

L LOCK-IN the meeting

Use what you learned from listening to your client and phrase your offer to them in a way that shows them the value of meeting with you. Then lock-in the meeting.

By remembering the **CALL** acronym, you will hit all the key elements of a successful call even when you feel the time pressure of an actual telephone call. We will explain each step of the **CALL** method later. For now, we just want you to know what it is and why we use it. So, we encourage you to...

...Use the CALL Method.

7

Build a CALL List

Build a CALL List

Proper Prior Preparation Produces a Powerful Performance

If you are like most people, you will feel some pressure when you get on the phone. This pressure can trigger your out-of-control personality responses. We find that carefully planning how to handle a potentially stressful situation can significantly reduce the stress. So, we suggest that you prepare for your telephone calls long before you pick up the phone.

We suggest that you prepare for your calls in three steps:

1. Build a call list
2. Write a call script
3. Practice the call script

This is the first of three chapters dedicated to your pre-**CALL** preparation. The suggestions in these three chapters will help you whether you make warm or cold calls. The principles apply in either case. Because cold calls present the biggest challenge for most sales people, the following comments presume a cold call scenario.

Build a CALL List

Who are you going to call? Before any phone call session, you must have a target list of prospects with as much information as possible on each one. Many people attempt to make phone calls by looking through their business card file, their PDA, their cell phone, or their planner. While this method yields some results, we have found much greater success when sales people work from an organized **CALL** list. In our experience, the greatest success comes when people enter a calling session with at least seventy-five names on their list.

You will achieve greater success working from a **CALL** list for several reasons:

- You can make more calls in less time if you do not have to look for numbers during the calling session.
- When you get the inevitable "no" (it happens to all of us), you will be able to maintain mental momentum by quickly moving to another call.
- You will get better at following your script as you move through the phone calling session if you don't have to stop to look for the next number between each call.
- The information about each contact on your **CALL** list can help you tailor your phone call to target their most likely problem or need.

Note: Learn how to build your **CALL** list every day. Discover how to get referrals from clients, friends, and associates – names with phone numbers. This subject is not our focus, but you can find many excellent resources on this topic. We recommend the book and audio program by Bob Burg – *Endless Referrals.*

CALL List Step 1: Define Your Target Market

We use three basic criteria to identify the best, or most likely market, for any given product or service. You can phrase these criteria in the form of questions.

Which companies, organizations, or people ...

... would be especially receptive to your product or service?

... would identify with you personally?

... are in a situation that naturally drives them to your product or service?

While many companies *could* benefit from using your product or service, not all *will*. To sharpen your focus and achieve greater success, invest some time on the front-end of the phone calling process by answering these three questions.

1 Which companies, organizations or people would be especially receptive to your product or service?

These companies, organizations, or people are ready to purchase before you walk in the door because:

- They know they need your product or service.
- They want to work with you.
- They don't flinch when you say how much it will cost.

Example: A company that you know by direct referral or that has some prior knowledge of the fit between their need and your offering. Let's say you sell incentive programs. A prospective client who overtly states their desire to implement a change in their employee recognition and reward program would fit in this category.

2 Which companies, organizations or people would identify with you personally?

People (your clients) buy products and services from other people (hopefully you). If you have some common background or experience with a group or the decision-maker for a group, you improve the odds of making the sale. Look for possible leads where you have existing connections or something in common with other people. Consider these possible sources:

- Local Chamber of Commerce
- Business networking groups
- High school or college Alumni newsletters
- Club, church or social organization rosters
- Trade or industry publications

3 Which companies, organizations or people are in a situation that naturally drives them to your product or service?

These companies have an overt problem that you can help them solve. For example:

- Declining profits
- Poor sales
- Stagnant growth
- Difficulty finding and retaining good employees
- High turnover
- Changes in customer requirements
- Declining market share
- Industry trends that threaten their market position

Here are some examples of target market statements:

- My target market is small business owners who want to reduce the conflict and stress within their teams.

- My target market is homeowners who want to reduce the time and effort they spend maintaining their yard.
- My target market is businesses in the hospitality industry who want to improve their customer retention.

CALL List Step 2: Combine all of your information into one place.

You want everything you need to know during a **CALL** session collected and recorded in one document.

Your CALL List should include (at a minimum):

1 Your target market definition statement

Do you sell to corporations or home owners? Do you target business owners or private individuals? Having this information in front of you when you call will help you get in the right mindset for the calling session. It may also assist you if you get stuck during the call. It can serve as a reminder to help you stay on track with your script.

2 Specific information about each contact:

- Business Name
- Contact Person
- Position
- Phone Numbers
- Email address
- Best time to call

You can get this information in many ways. Read corporate reports. Snoop around on the internet. Talk to clients of your clients. Check websites, brochures, articles written about them, etc. You can REALLY impress a client with a little work before you call or visit them.

Here is one example of what you can do to make a great first impression. Many company websites have photos and/or bios of employees. Check their website and memorize the names and faces of key people before you meet them. Then, when you have the opportunity to meet face-to-face, address them by name before you are formally introduced.

Although this may seem like a lot of background busy-work, this effort will help you gain the attention of decision-makers. In addition to arming you to impress the decision-maker, your research may also reveal additional potential clients.

> **Remember:** Your clients care more about their needs than they do about you or your product.

Your **CALL** list should include any information you might need to quickly connect with your prospective clients. Your research will prepare you to immediately show them how what you offer can improve their situation.

3 **Name of the decision-maker (if they are not your initial contact)**

4 **Name of the "Gatekeeper" – the person who controls access to the decision-maker. (You may not initially know this person's name.)**

5 **Ten questions you can ask to help you connect with and understand your client**

Ideally, you can customize the ten questions to each individual client's situation. But, even if you cannot customize completely, having 10 basic questions before you start your calls will help you get going much faster. You will probably not use all of the questions on your initial phone call with any given client. For most calls, you may use only 2 or 3 of them. By having more questions than you need, you will project more confidence than if you try to think of the questions during the call.

For example , you could ask questions like...

- How satisfied are you with...
- How concerned are you about...
- Is this a concern for...
- Are you experiencing challenges with...

> **Warning:** "What can you tell me about your company?" would not be a good question. This question indicates that you know little or nothing about their concerns and that you expect them to teach you how to serve them. You want to come across as the expert, not as a rookie.

So, we encourage you to...

...Build a CALL List

8

Write a CALL Script

Write a CALL Script

As simple as this idea sounds, it still yields powerful results. When you write a **CALL** script, you have pre-planned your conversation with the decision-maker so that you clearly answer your prospective client's unspoken question – "Why are you calling me?" With this pre-planning, you significantly improve your odds of success.

We recommend that you invest the time to write a well thought-out script that you intend to use on the phone. If you have a script, you will feel less pressure when you place your calls.

Let's get Joe's perspective on this point:

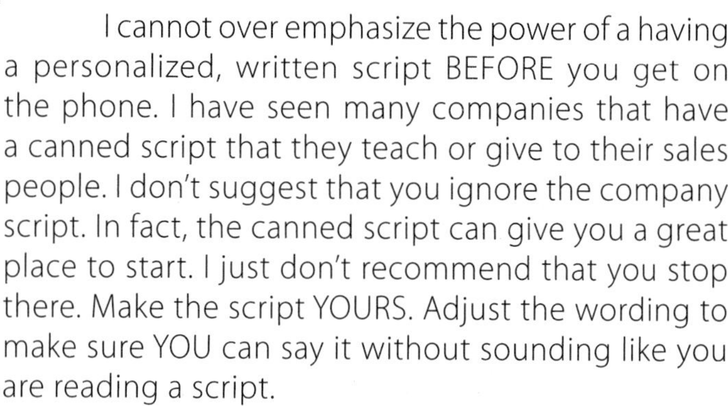

I cannot over emphasize the power of a having a personalized, written script BEFORE you get on the phone. I have seen many companies that have a canned script that they teach or give to their sales people. I don't suggest that you ignore the company script. In fact, the canned script can give you a great place to start. I just don't recommend that you stop there. Make the script YOURS. Adjust the wording to make sure YOU can say it without sounding like you are reading a script.

Your script should answer your client's first question, "Why are you calling me?" And, it should include two parts:

1. Your Elevator Speech (modified for the phone)
2. Your invitation or offer

CALL Script Step 1: Your Elevator Speech

Ten seconds of Triumph or… Tragedy!

As you develop your script, remember that your prospective client may or may not know what you do and why you are calling. If the person on the other end of the phone does not know you well, they will tend to get uncomfortable with the call quickly. To prepare yourself for this situation, develop a quick personal introduction as part of your script.

Many sales and networking trainers call this introduction your "elevator speech" because you should be able to say it quickly and smoothly in less than 10 seconds – about the time it takes you to talk with someone on an elevator.

Here is what you should cover in your elevator speech:

- Who you are
- What company you represent
- What your company does (your product or service)
- The BENEFIT of your product or service

In other words, your elevator speech should at least partially answer your client's question, "Why are you calling me?"

In addition to answering your client's first question, your elevator speech should also help you identify and qualify good candidates for your products or services. Spending time with people uninterested in what you offer is definitely not your goal. You only want to present your offer to people who can benefit from AND want what you offer. Since people tend to buy for emotional reasons and then justify their decisions with logical reasons, you want to target emotion first and logic second.

> **Note:** Remember the **Model of Human Behavior** (Appendix 2)? About 35% of the population is task-oriented, and about 65% of the population is people-oriented. Based on these percentages, you can safely assume that about 65% of the people you speak to will rely on emotion first and logic second. Since everyone is a blend of both Task and People orientation, even Task-oriented people have an emotional side. So, the odds of connecting with a person based on emotion are actually higher than 65%. Since you may not know much about the person on the other end of the phone yet, put the odds in your favor. **Go with emotion first.**

Your benefit statement should connect with the emotion behind your product or service. We will cover more specifics in a moment, but just to clarify our point for now:

- Notice that a common statement like, "I sell cleaning supplies," offers a service.
- While something like, "I reduce the expense of cleaning and improve the appearance and safety of your building," connects with an emotion.

> **Note:** While networking and meeting new people is not the topic of this book, you can use your elevator speech for this purpose as well.

The elevator speech separates the men from the boys (or the girls from the women). With a great elevator speech, you will project a confident, knowledgeable professionalism. With a poor one, you will crash and burn like many amateurish sales people.

You will use your elevator speech almost every time you speak with someone for the first time. This could happen on a cold call or in a face-to-face meeting at a leads group/networking meeting, a Chamber of Commerce event, or at a social gathering.

Your elevator speech should spark interest in speaking with you further – you do not want it to sell your product or service. Too often, overly anxious sales people feel that business has to happen now or never. As a result, their elevator speech sounds more like a pitch about themselves, their company and their product or service than it sounds like a sincere answer to a question. If you use this approach, you will fail more often than you succeed because your potential client will feel pushed or chased. No one likes to feel pushed or chased.

This sales pitch type of elevator speech happens because many sales people operate under the "close the deal" definition of sales that we discussed under Bogus Belief #1. As a result, they think that the elevator speech should answer the question, "What do you do?" In fact, the elevator speech should actually answer the client's question, "What problem can you solve for me?"

Let's look at some elevator speeches we have heard in the past:

A *"Hi, I'm ________ and I represent ________ company from San Diego, CA. We offer a large line of swimming pool products, accessories and pool toys. Kids just love our new volleyball set. We also offer pool pumps, pool filters, and training for our clients. I would love to get together with you and show you our cost comparisons."*

B *"We do landscape design. We have the time for your design. Let us make your backyard fine."*

C *"We're a sales consultancy specializing in visioning, team building, strategy development, and interaction dynamics."*

Each of these three examples answers the question, "What do you do?" (And, the rhyme in B is just plain awful!)

Prospective clients care about the problem you can solve for them. They don't really care what you do. Make sure that your first statement tells your prospective client: *Why they should invest their time talking with you.* That is their main concern, so tell them. You only have about 10-20 seconds. Lead with the results your offer delivers for them.

Let's look at each of the elevator speeches again to apply this principle and discover some valuable hints for creating your own speech.

Elevator Speech A

Original Statement:

"Hi, I'm _____________ and I represent _____________ company from San Diego, CA. We offer a large line of swimming pool products, accessories and pool toys. Kids just love our new volleyball set . We also offer pool pumps, pool filters, and training for our clients. I would love to get together with you and show you our cost comparisons."

Comment:

This speech yells, "LOOK AT ME AND MY STUFF!" This blatant approach causes prospective clients to shut down because it sends the completely self-serving message that, "I WANT TO MAKE MONEY FROM YOU!"

Remember, clients want solutions for their challenges.

Giving too much information in too little time can project a fast-talking, untrustworthy image.

Here is a stronger statement:

"We increase profit margins for pool companies by providing high quality products at reduced wholesale costs."

Notice we are beginning with an attention getter – "We increase profit margins." Your prospective client will probably ask for more information.

Hint #1 Lead with a focus on your client's needs. Do not emphasize yourself or your offerings. You can answer these questions later.

Hint #2 Solve your client's problem.

Hint #3 Keep it short enough that you can say it with calm confidence.

Hint #4 Remember you are speaking with a busy individual – get to the point.

Elevator Speech B

Original Statement:

"We do landscape design. We have the time for your design. Let us make your backyard fine." (Ughhh!)

Comment:

As awful as this is, we have actually heard and read statements like this one.

Rhymes sound trite and amateurish. They seldom get the professional attention you desire.

Here is a stronger statement:

"We take the back-breaking work out of lawn and garden care at an affordable price."

Here we highlight the prospective client's "pain" – "We take the back-breaking work out of..."

Hint #5 Find the pain and highlight it.

Hint #6 Save the rhymes for your love letters.

Elevator Speech C

Original statement:

"We're a sales consultancy specializing in visioning, team building, strategy development, and interaction dynamics."

Comment:

This statement not only lists offerings rather than solutions, it also does it in a complex and confusing manner. Remember, even CEO's (and everyone else in an organization) are people. Regardless of your contact person's position within the company, you are still speaking with a human being.

Here is a stronger statement:

"We provide new ideas and assistance to companies that want to improve customer retention and decrease employee turnover."

This statement forms a strong connection because it offers new ideas and assistance to meet a clearly defined need.

Hint #7 Choose words that will connect with your client and clarify your benefit statement. Avoid complicated statements that might confuse or frustrate your prospective client.

Hint #8 Words like *ideas*, *assistance* and *improve* create value and will often connect with decision-makers.

As you craft your sentence or two, remember to lead with the results that your prospective client wants to achieve.

In other words: create an elevator speech designed to…

> ***Find and offer a solution to your client's unsolved problem or unmet need.***

Identifying the Right Words for Your Elevator Speech

You can identify the right words to target your client's "hot button" – their unsolved problem or unmet need – by looking in two places:

1 Your past success

When you solicit comments and testimonials from past clients, they will help you determine what people see as your most valuable product or service.

What problems do you solve? Why do your past clients praise your product or service? Use exit interviews, testimonials, and customer comments to help you see your offering from your current clients' (and therefore your future clients') perspective.

2 Industry trends

The information and data you gain from looking into current industry trends will better define the significance of your offerings and help you to differentiate yourself in the market.

Listen to what Joe and Dawn have to say on this topic:

Our business took off when we listened to our past clients. We specialize in sales training, live phone contacting, team building, conflict resolution, etc. Because we can work in so many different situations and with such a broad client base, we initially struggled to briefly define a value statement to give our elevator speech power.

As our business developed, we read our client testimonials and comments. After a while, we started to see a recurring theme. At the conclusion of our training, employers reported greater employee engagement and productivity.

From this observation, we created the following value statement (slogan, tagline, etc): *Accomplish more with the staff you have in place.* The concise nature of this value statement does two things. It gives decision-makers an idea they can wrap their minds around, and it solves a problem many business owners and managers want to solve.

Using this value statement, we created this elevator speech, "*We help you accomplish more with the staff you have in place.*"

CALL Script Step 2: Your Invitation or Offer

Simply put, you call people to either schedule an appointment or to move them off of your prospective client list. Your invitation or offer should target this purpose. You do not want to explain everything, make your sales presentation, or close the sale in the phone call. If your prospective client has a need that you can fill, you want to get an appointment. We believe that every phone call should end with one of three definite outcomes:

1. They either do not qualify for your offer or they have no interest in further discussion
2. You schedule a confirmed time for a follow-up phone conversation, or
3. You schedule a confirmed time and place for a face-to-face meeting.

In our experience, sending additional information without an agreed to follow-up discussion creates a sales-person-chasing the-prospect situation. As a result, we do not list that option as an acceptable phone call outcome. If you construct your script properly and follow thorough on your execution of it, you will come to one of the three viable outcomes nearly every time you place a call.

Once you have introduced yourself, you need to explain your offer in a way that makes sense to your prospective client. Complicated offers confuse people, and confused people always say "no." In the next few pages, we will elaborate further on how you can adapt this step for each client. For now, remember the general concept that you should keep the invitation or offer short and sweet. For example:

- "Why don't we schedule a brief appointment?"

- "I would like to offer you a free cleanliness survey of your facility."
- "I am calling today to schedule a time when we can meet briefly."

Use your own words, but make it specific. In general, calling to offer information will not move you closer to a meeting. You can be ready with additional information if asked, but do not make that the purpose of your call. You are calling to *schedule an appointment*.

CALL Script Step 3: Put The Elevator Speech and the Invitation Together to Create Your Written Script

For clarity sake, we will make this point again: you will save both time and money if you will learn to use the telephone effectively. As part of this process, we promote, and highly recommend, that you use a customized script to open the conversation with your prospect.

So far, we have covered the two components of a general script. Now we will put them together in what we call a customized script. Many people respond to this statement with a look of confusion and ask: "What is a customized script?"

A general script contains the key elements that you intend to discuss with every client. It guides you so that you make an effective and efficient contact. You customize the script when you adapt your elevator speech and your offer to the specific needs (which you discovered during your pre-**CALL** research) of each prospective client. Ultimately, you want to develop a script that comes across as natural and conversational, not stiff and formal.

At the risk of sounding redundant, we will state the number one rule of effective sales:

> *Focus on your client's needs and not on your needs.*

If you do this, you will stand out from the other sales people who call on both your current and prospective clients. When you call for an appointment (especially on a cold call), you want to stand out and catch your client's attention. So, your script needs to reflect your knowledge of them and your concern for their situation.

The following is a good telephone script, but it could be better.

> *"Hello, Mr. Smith, my name is Bill Jones. I am a Facility Consultant with XYZ Janitorial and Cleaning Supply. We specialize in reducing the labor and materials cost of cleaning services, while improving the appearance and cleanliness of your building. We would gladly do a free cleanliness survey to assist you in your facility maintenance efforts. I am calling today to schedule a brief appointment with you. Do you have your calendar available?"*

The positives here are:

- the caller introduced himself
- the script leads with the solution to a problem.

Unfortunately, this script sounds stiff and formal like the scripts used by most telemarketers. It leaves no room for your client to speak. Rather than create a long statement that you read to your prospective client, we recommend that you create a script *outline* that helps you to stay on topic and be engaging at the same time. When you engage someone in a directed conversation, you will begin the process of connecting with them on a personal level.

Many sales people have a tendency to rattle on, telling their story without stopping for breath. They sound as if they are afraid that the client will brush them off before they have had the chance to deliver their pitch. This often happens because they want to close the deal. When they shift their thinking to solving the customer's problem, they can slow down and relax. We recommend that you take the latter approach.

To sound natural, and unrushed as you speak with your prospective clients, we suggest that you follow a *directed discussion* approach rather than a *data dump* approach. When you follow a directed discussion script, you will separate yourself from other sales people. Create a directed discussion script outline using the flow of the **CALL** method.

CONNECT with the person on the phone

1. INTRODUCE YOURSELF (use your elevator speech here)
2. CLEAR THE TIME. Ask the client if this is a good time to talk. If they say that they are busy, ask for another time to call. Distracted people do not listen very well. Be sensitive to whether or not the client sounds busy. Recognize that High-**S** clients will often say it is okay, when they are really too busy to talk.
3. ESTABLISH PERSONAL CREDIBILITY.
    - If you have a referral, here is the place to use it.
        - Joe Miller asked me to give you a call. (Weak)
        - Joe Miller said you're the man I need to connect with. (Better)
        - We just helped Joe Miller reduce his costs and he said you might want to get the same results. (Strong)

- Mention a market trend or situation that is relevant to this particular company. "I noticed your corporate report mentioned that you are actively seeking ways to reduce the cost of ..."

A ANSWER the unspoken question, "Why are you calling me?"

Engage the client in a directed conversation – i.e. a conversation that you direct. How do you do that? Simple, just ask one of the 10 questions that you created on your **CALL** list. As much as possible, personalize the phrasing of your questions to fit your client's situation (industry, location, number of employees, etc.)

As you grow in your ability to read their personality style (Chapter 11), you can also customize your approach based on their style. You may not know your client's exact personality style, but you might have some indication of it from your research or prior contact with them. If you have this information, use the following ideas to customize your questions. For the...

- D **High-D client** - ask direct, bottom-line questions
- I **High-I client** - ask friendly, conversational questions; let them talk.
- S **High-S client** - use soft vocal tones to ask non-confrontational questions and wait for them to answer.
- C **High-C client** - ask questions that call for factual (as opposed to feeling) answers, avoid getting too personal, and (like **S**'s) wait for them to answer.

While your goal at this stage of the conversation is to answer their unspoken question, you want to be the one actually asking the questions.

Remember this key point: The person asking the questions controls the direction of the conversation.

If you have created good questions (and you exercise the next step well) you will uncover their pain and show them the benefit of investing a few moments with you. While you do not have to specifically state the purpose of your call, you should demonstrate value to them by the way you ask questions and listen to the answers.

L LISTEN to their response

1. LISTEN to how they answer your questions. You will have to STOP TALKING to do this. In our experience, poor listening skills hurt more sales people than nearly anything else. Frankly, listening takes more effort than most people are willing to expend. When you master the art of listening, you will move from taking orders from clients to making orders happen.

2. TAKE NOTES – Pay particular attention to the comments they make that can tie into your offering.

    - Are they having any difficulties?
    - What are their concerns?
    - What frustrates them most?
    - Which elements are they just lukewarm about?
    - What have they tried to do to rectify this situation?

- What is their voice tone and pace? Are they outgoing or reserved?
- Are they more focused on *thinking* (data, numbers, results) or *feeling* (people, who referred you, relationships)? Are they task or people oriented?

3 As appropriate, follow their answers with more specific questions targeted at uncovering their unsolved problem or unmet need (their pain).

The first concern the client mentions is rarely their REAL concern or pain. You will probably have to do some digging. Remember to stop short of frustrating or annoying them with too many questions. You want to schedule an appointment, not make a sales presentation. You only need to find out if they have a pain that you can help to eliminate. You do not need every detail at this point. Guide the direction of the conversation with your questions, and let them set the tone for how long the conversation lasts.

We go into more detail on the Probing and Clarifying process in **Sell Naked In Person.**

L **LOCK-IN** the meeting

1 OFFER your product or service as a way to fix the problem they mentioned if it actually does fix their problem. If not, have integrity. Get off the phone and don't take any more of their time.

2 BOOK THE APPOINTMENT! – You can do this with either:

- ***a question*** - "Why don't we get together next Friday to discuss this further?", or
- ***a statement*** - "It sounds like we should meet to discuss this further."

Base your choice of a question or a statement on the tone and direction of the conversation. How you do it matters less than remembering to do it. If they qualify for your offer, schedule a firm time and date to meet again. You will virtually eliminate no shows and cancellations if you say something like: "I'm marking my calendar for ________. I plan to be there. Is this a firm appointment? I will be traveling an hour to meet with you."

> **Caution:** If possible, avoid booking meetings on Mondays. These are high cancellation days.

As you move through your script, remember the power of asking questions to engage your prospective client.

Joe has a great story to illustrate the value of using questions to probe the client's needs during the phone call.

I remember one conversation I had with the Vice President of Sales for one of my clients. He kept putting up a pretty good front by saying that his sales team was doing fine. I almost politely ended the call so that I could get on with my next call. Then it occurred to me that he stayed engaged and conversational. So, I decided to ask more detailed questions. When I asked a question about territory management, he blurted out, "The problem with my sales staff is that their territory runs them! They are wasting time and gas running all over the area."

"Really?" I replied. "What methods have you used to rectify this situation?"

In his answer, he spoke at length about the various ideas he had tried. None of them had been effective.

I let him fully vent his frustration over this problem. Then I said, "It seems to me that what I do might be a help to you as this is a situation I've had a great deal of success with in the past. How about we set up a time to get together so I can run a few **ideas** by you? Is there anyone else you would like to have in the meeting?"

When I uncovered his pain and offered him a way to eliminate it, he immediately agreed to a meeting.

Notice how Joe handled this situation:

- He skillfully used questions to elicit a pain response.
- He listened patiently.
- He used a key word (ideas) to improve the odds of a positive response.
- He confidently moved from conversation to scheduling an appointment.
- He asked about other people who might be involved in the decision-making process.

Joe's example in the story above clearly demonstrates two key concepts we have already covered. First, the value of knowing yourself and what tends to push you to an out-of-control response. And second, the value of preparation prior to the call.

Joe has a very strong **D**-type personality style. Listening to people vent their frustrations can create stress for Joe because he has a drive for quick results. He has worked diligently to develop the ability to control his desire to push the conversation to a conclusion when other people are talking. The way he let his client vent his frustration shows the incredible self-control that Joe has developed. By controlling his own response, he created a better connection with his client and found his client's real concern.

Because he knew where he wanted the conversation to go and had practiced the skills in advance, he knew what to do when the conversation began to stall. He used a script to get the conversation started and then one of the questions he uses to move conversations forward. Because he had prepared, he was able to find his client's need despite the initial lukewarm response to his call.

Once he found his client's need, he immediately offered his services as a way to eliminate the pain. He offered no extra discussion and no over-the-top self-promotion. He just used a friendly, business-like move into scheduling the meeting to discuss ideas that could help his client.

When you master these concepts you will, like Joe and Dawn, book more meetings and make more sales. So, we encourage you to...

...Write a CALL Script

9

Prepare for the Inevitable – Objections

Prepare for the Inevitable – Objections

As a first step in preparing for objections, write two or three different variations of your elevator speech so that you will have different ways to say the same thing already prepared before you get on the phone. You will need different ways to say essentially the same thing as you handle objections. Having different versions of your elevator speech prepares you with ways to rephrase or clarify your statement if your first approach does not connect with your client. For instance, Joe and Dawn might say, "I help companies accomplish more with the staff they have in place," OR they can say, "I help teams that are struggling with communication issues."

As the next step, anticipate possible objections and plan some answers for them. Since you know that the objections will come, you should prepare for them in advance.

Addressing Common Objections to Scheduling a Meeting

By opening your conversations in a way that minimizes objections, you achieve greater success in sales. For example, when you lead with statements such as:

- "I've surveyed a few of your customers and ..."
- "I have been studying your business and ..."
- "In my research concerning your quarterly report I learned ..."

you are less likely to hear:

- "We're not interested."
- "We are happy with the service we are currently receiving."
- "Call me in 6 months."

- "I don't want to waste your time or mine."
- "Do you have any materials you can send me?"

If you start the conversation the right way, people will probably be curious to know what comments you received from their customers or what you have learned by studying their business.

However, even with a well thought out elevator speech, a perfect script, and excellent phone technique, you will still encounter some objections as you call to schedule meetings.

Whole books have been written about techniques for overcoming objections, so that is not our primary focus here. We have found, though, that anticipating the likely objections you will face and pre-planning an approach for addressing them improves your success rate.

In an effort to share some thoughts on how to address the most common objections, we have included some possible responses below. We do not propose that this section covers every possibility, but we do believe we have given you some valuable insights to improve your success. In **Sell Naked In Person** we cover handling objections in more detail as part of the process of closing the sale.

General Principles for Handling Objections

As you read these possible responses, notice the key thoughts behind every response:

- Agree with your prospective client's perspective – arguing will not help.
- Emphasize that you only want to schedule a short meeting – no more than 15 minutes.
- Redirect the objection so that meeting with you will help them in some way – again, arguing will not help.

- Personalize your response to the client and the situation. Canned responses sound that way, and they tend to irritate people.

Specific Tips for Handling Objections

Savvy decision-makers may respond to your opening statement with one of the following:

1 "What are you selling?"

Stay focused on your benefit statement! Don't regurgitate your list of product and/or service offerings. Use one of the variations of your elevator speech like:

- We help companies who are struggling with…
- We increase profit margins…
- We help companies decrease turnover …
- We work to streamline efficiency….

2 "We're not interested."

First, agree with them. When you validate their position, they may be more willing to listen to you. Argue your point, and you will fail (miserably). You could say something like:

Mr. Jones, I understand that you may not be interested at this time. The reason I'd like to meet with you is to give you a few ideas that may assist you as you grow your company. I will be in your area next week. Could we set up a 15 minute appointment?

-or-

Mr. Jones, I realize that you are not interested at this time. The reason I would like to meet with you is to share some information I've learned in my research that may assist you in your efforts to increase your profits. I will be in your area next week. Could we set up a 15 minute appointment?

3 "Send me information." Or, "Do you have material you could send to me?"

This statement may provide you with a clue to their personality style. Many High-**S** type decision-makers will say something like this because they do not want to tell you "no." Many High-**C** decision-makers might say this because they want to check you out before meeting with you. Most **D** and **I** type decision-makers will not say this because they don't want to take the time to review your information. They will probably decide immediately whether or not they want to meet with you.

To address this objection, attempt to redirect the conversation. For example, you could explain that your company specializes in customizing for the specific needs of the client. Or you might explain that you have found that written information will not do your company or theirs justice. Assuming one or both of these statements is true, you could then tell them that to accurately assess your ability to help them, you need the kind of information that only a face-to-face meeting can provide. Then reiterate a version of your script. For example:

Mr. Jones we have built our business on specializing our products to meet the needs of each customer. In fact, we have so much literature on so many different products that it would not serve you well for me to send information that might not be of value. If you could give me 15 minutes of your time, we could decide what information I should leave you. My goal is to give you exactly what you want. Could we check our calendars and set an appointment?

4 "I'm too busy."

If you have scripted properly, you will only hear this objection from someone who is truly too busy. Every industry has its hectic times. The end of the month and the end of the quarter are usually not great times to call a retail sales company for an appointment.

School districts are busy at the beginning and end of the school year. Non-profit and faith-based organizations are busiest around the holidays.

If you get this objection, handle it by agreeing with them and then gently reminding them that you called them *because they are busy*. Explain that you know they are busy and that from your study of their business you know that they will be just as busy, if not more, in two months or two years. Tell them that you want to save them time, and that is why it would be beneficial to them for you to meet within the next few weeks. For example:

Mr. Jones, I know you are busy. In fact, that's why I called. I think that our ______________ will help you save time doing ______________ so that you're not still this busy two years from now. If you can give me fifteen minutes, I promise that you will have the information to decide if we can help you save money and increase your profit margin. If I'm any longer than fifteen minutes it will be because you ask me to stay. Let's look at our calendars and set a date.

5 "We don't have money in the budget. Call us back later."

This statement quite possibly is true. However, if you wait too long to schedule an initial meeting, you may find that they still don't have the money because they will have forgotten about you.

Recognize that you may have called them in the middle of their fiscal year, and that they are not prepared for this opportunity. Again, agree with them. Help them admit that companies often do not have enough money in the budget for the things they really need. Then tell them the benefit of meeting now rather than later. If your product or service will save them time or money in the long run, tell them. Your testimonials from other companies will often help in this situation. Here is an example:

Mr. Jones, I completely understand. I know that you are right in the middle of your fiscal year, and you didn't plan for this expenditure. In fact, many of the other companies that we have helped started their relationship with us in the same situation. In many of those other situations, we found that we had to start the planning process long before the fiscal year started so that we could help them solve ____________. Why don't we get together to see specifically what you need so that I can draw up a proposal . That way, you will have an accurate idea of how much to budget next year.

To make this approach really powerful, you could cite a specific client story in this example rather than make a general statement.

6 "We already do business with company X."

This objection has the potential to take the wind out of your sails. Don't let it. Unless your company has an exclusive product or service, your prospective client is *probably* doing business with someone else.

Agree with them that company X is a great company and then explain the benefits you can offer that differentiate you from them. Testimonials may work here. If you can find something to offer that company X does not offer, you may be able to get your foot in the door so that you can build a stronger relationship with the client. For example:

Mr. Jones, Company X does a great job at what they do. In fact, some of my other clients also work with them for some of their products. I do believe we have some specialized products/services that will improve your bottom line. Mr. Jones, would it be worth fifteen minutes of your time to see if we can help you?

7 **"I don't want to waste your time or mine."**

You will most likely get this comment when your opening statement misses the mark for the client. So, redirect and try again. Remember to agree with them. You might say something like:

Mr. Jones, I agree with you about wasting time. I don't like to waste time either. In fact, I called because I thought that I could save you time and money and increase your profit margins in the future. I'd just like to meet with you to find out if this is true. My market research shows that we can help you save time and money. Would it be worth fifteen minutes of your time to see if we can assist your company?

You can (and should) modify each of these approaches according to what you understand about your prospective client based on your knowledge of the **Model of Human Behavior**. We cover this topic in greater detail in **Sell Naked In Person**. For now, though, we encourage you to...

...Prepare for Objections

10

Practice the CALL Script

Practice the CALL Script

To become comfortable with the script, practice it before you use it in a live phone call.

Here is Joe's perspective on practicing your **CALL** script:

To practice your call script, I recommend reading it into a recording device. Your voicemail, digital recorder, or PDA will do. Once you record it, you can listen to your inflections, pauses, and volume. Listening to your recording helps you hear what your client hears so that you can make adjustments in your delivery. This step can dramatically improve your learning curve.

Once you are comfortable with the flow of the script and you have practiced it privately a few times, do role-play exercises with another person. I have done enough of these sessions to know what many of you might be thinking right now. Outgoing people (**D** and **I** types) probably think, "What a waste of time! Can't we just get started?" Reserved people (**C** and **S** types) probably think, "I'm not sure I want to do this with another person. I'm not comfortable with this idea." Remember – reframe your fear, apprehension, or skepticism in a way that motivates you to do what you need to do. Here is a way to reframe some common concerns:

D **High-D's** – "If I slow down long enough to practice, my calls will get better results."

I **High-I's** – "If I focus long enough to practice, I'll have more fun with people when I'm on the phone."

S **High-S's** – "If I'm willing to practice this script with someone else, I'll feel more comfortable with it and I'll know what to expect when I make client calls."

C **High-C's** – "If I sit down with another person for a few minutes and allow them to give me feedback, I'll be better prepared to make these calls correctly when they really count."

The bottom line is this (yes, I'm going **D** on you), I have never seen anyone in all of my sales training experience who didn't improve their call effectiveness by doing some role-play practice before they used their script. Regardless of your prior experience level, role-playing a script can help you improve – particularly if you haven't used the adaptive approaches we suggest.

I have found that role-play practice can help you become comfortable using the script and adjusting to the client once you are on the phone. In my training sessions, I often take the part of the customer to help sales people practice their part. At a minimum, I suggest that you do some back-and-forth role-play with another sales person before you actually get on the phone with prospective clients.

To get the most out of the role-play practice, give each other some tough questions and objections so that you get used to addressing them in a controlled environment. I also suggest that the person playing

the part of the client take on different personality traits so that the person placing the call can practice adapting to the client. (We will go into more detail about how to adapt to different clients later.)

Many people dread role-play because they fear public humiliation. In fact, I used to dread it myself. I have learned that if you keep it light-hearted and fun, this fear will go away so that you can prepare for success. You don't want to beat each other up in this session. The goal of the role-play is to build confidence and to practice the adaptive skills we will discuss later.

Once you feel comfortable with the script, do the role-play exercises. You will radically improve your results.

So, we encourage you to...

...Practice your CALL Script

"Success...seems to be connected with action. Successful men keep moving. They make mistakes, but they don't quit."

- Conrad Hilton

11

Building Rapport -
Bridging the Broken Bonds of Trust

Building Rapport

Bridging the Broken Bonds of Trust

Once you reach someone on the phone, you need to quickly overcome their likely skepticism. They may be naturally skeptical people, but more likely they have learned skepticism from past experiences with other sales people who use the close the deal approach to sales. So, how do you do overcome skepticism? We suggest that you attempt to come across in a way that invites your prospect to like you so that you can build rapport with them.

As a sales professional, you may have already heard that you need to build rapport with your clients. Just to make sure that we work from the same understanding of this concept, we will begin with some definitions and observations.

The American Heritage Dictionary defines rapport as:

> relationship, especially one of mutual trust
> or emotional affinity.

Effective sales people know how to establish rapport with their prospects and clients. They understand this general rule:

> ***We tend to connect with and like people who are similar to us.***

Ultimately you want to reach the rapport stage in relationship with your clients. However, you will not likely reach that level of connection in the first phone conversation. During the sales call, target a friendly connection so that you have the opportunity to meet with your prospective client. The first sale you make will be the sale that gets you the appointment. When using the phone, you only have a few sentences to make this connection.

Remember, most decisions – especially buying decisions – are first emotion based and then supported by logic. If you connect with your prospective client on the phone, you will book more meetings. When you book more meetings, you make more sales. So, develop the skill of connecting with people over the phone.

Notice that we use the word "skill" to describe this ability. Every personality style has both strengths that help them build connections and blind spots that limit their ability to connect with others. Regardless of your personality style, you can learn the skill of connecting with people. Once you make a connection, you can then work on building rapport.

The process of building rapport varies with the person, but we do notice some patterns. We can look at the process from two different perspectives: task-oriented and people-oriented. The process of building rapport follows the general flow shown below.

The Rapport Building Process

Task-oriented individuals tend to move through these steps as they go from the initial connection to a state of rapport.

Connect => Trust => Relationship => Rapport

People-oriented individuals tend to follow the same steps, but in a different order.

Connect => Relationship => Trust => Rapport

We owe our understanding of the above process to Jean Brun – our Behavior Symptoms Analysis expert. We will learn more from Jean (we know him as JJ) in **Sell Naked In Person**. We could easily dedicate a full chapter to the rapport-building process, but that is not our intent here. For now, let's see what initial insights we can learn from the general rapport-building process.

First, notice that the rapport process always begins with a connection. At the connection stage, your prospective client starts to *think* (if they are task-oriented) or *feel* (if they are people-oriented) that they like you. This thought or feeling will most likely start because they see a part of themselves in you. Remember the general rule:

> ***We tend to connect with and like people who are similar to us.***

The next steps in the process depend on your prospective client's primary drive.

Building Rapport with Task-oriented Individuals

For most task-oriented individuals, after making a connection, their next thought in the process of building rapport focuses on trust. In looking at you, they often ask themselves these questions:

- "Can I trust this person to do what they promise?"
- "Can I trust this person's information?"
- "Can I trust that this person is honest and truthful?"
- "Can I trust that this person will respect my time?"
- "Can I trust that this person will be logical?"

Once they decide that they can trust you, they are more likely to take the initial connection deeper to a relationship stage. From the relationship stage, they may be willing to move to the deeper level of rapport.

Building Rapport with People-oriented Individuals

For most people-oriented individuals, after making a connection, their next step in the rapport-building process will come from how they feel about you. In deciding if they can move with you to a friendly relationship level, they may ask themselves questions like:

- "Does this person care about me?"
- "Does this person genuinely like me?"
- "Do I feel good about this person?"
- "How does this person treat other people?"
- "Will this person listen to me?"

Once they decide that they feel good about you, they then observe how the relationship develops (how you interact with them and others) to decide if they can trust you. When they reach the trust stage, they may be willing to move to the deeper level of rapport.

The rapport-building process has many implications that lie outside the scope of this book. For now, we just want to gain some initial insights into what really happens in this process and to recognize that the process changes from person to person depending on their blend of task and people traits.

For the purposes of this book, we want to introduce the concept of the rapport-building process and give you some background information to use in your phone **CALL** sessions. The rapport-building process has greater significance in face-to-face meetings than it does in any brief telephone conversation. We offer the information here so that you have a starting point for understanding the different perspectives people often take with regard to building rapport.

We think that you should notice the flow so that you can better understand your client's perspective. For now, though, we want to turn your attention to the first step of the **CALL** method and the first step in building rapport – CONNECT with the person on the phone.

Making a Connection

You probably only have a few seconds of interaction during your initial phone call. So, what do you do? You cannot possibly assess the exact style blend of the person on the other end of the phone in such a short time. So, we recommend that you listen for, and respond to, what you hear in the other person's voice. You do this in two steps.

Connection Step 1: Listen for vocal pace and volume

If they speak quickly and loudly, they are probably more outgoing. If they speak slowly and softly, they are probably more reserved. If their pace and volume matches your natural pace and volume, great. You will probably connect fairly well. If you notice that you speak at a different pace and volume from them, just adjust to match them.

To develop a connection quickly, practice matching the mood, pitch, speed and volume of your prospective client. When people hear themselves in your voice, they tend to like you.

Connection Step 2: Decide if they are task or people oriented

Once you have made a guess about whether they are more outgoing or reserved, you then try to decide if they are more task-oriented or people-oriented. This difference may not be immediately obvious. So, here is what we recommend: go with the odds. *Initially assume that they are people-oriented and go for an emotional connection.*

We recommend that you start with feeling words rather than thinking words because most of your clients will tend to be more people-oriented than task-oriented. If your discussion continues for very long, you can listen for your prospective client's primary driver as well.

Task-oriented people tend to say things like:

- "I think that..."
- "It seems to me that..."
- "How can I get more information about..."

People-oriented types tend to say things like:

- "I feel that…"
- "I'm not comfortable with…"
- "Who else can I speak to about…"

Many people ask the question, "What if they're task-oriented and you start the conversation with feeling words? Won't you miss the connection by assuming that they are people-oriented?" The short answer is: probably not.

If they are primarily task-oriented, they most likely have a strong people-oriented secondary trait. So, the odds of irritating them by attempting to connect on a feeling basis are low. In fact, if they have a very strong task nature, they might not even notice that you used a feeling, emotional approach. If you notice any disconnect at this point, just adjust your wording to a task/thinking basis. The point is this – put the odds in your favor to start the conversation and then adjust as necessary.

If you know the person you are calling, by all means go with what you know about them and tailor your approach accordingly. The suggestion above assumes that you do not know the person. Just based on the odds (65% of people are people-oriented), you will be right more than you are wrong if you go for emotion first.

Putting it together, you will probably note the following in your phone conversations:

D **High-D clients** – short, direct discussion with little small talk, probably decisive and quick to state an opinion

I **High-I clients** – friendly, expressive conversation, probably willing to talk freely

- S **High-S clients** – friendly, soft conversation, probably listens more than they talk
- C **High-C clients** – short, precise, conversation, they may question you more than they state their position; likely to be cautious about making commitments

You see, this isn't rocket science. You just have to be aware of the differences and adjust your behaviors accordingly. Listen to your prospective client's word choice, vocal tones, and pace of speech then adjust yours to fit them.

This information will help you adjust your phone conversations and target your sales presentations to address your client's needs and concerns.

When you understand your style blend, and learn to identify and appreciate your client's style blend, you will communicate more effectively and connect with people more often.

Note: You can grow your skills in the area of identifying your prospective client's personality style with role-play exercises. If you have other team members with different personality styles, you can have them coach you on how to adjust to clients of their style. You can also coach them on how to adjust to clients of your style.

Very important point: Adjusting to fit another person's style can help you build a connection, but never try to duplicate a regional or national accent. You will probably sound like you are mocking them and that would have a negative result.

12

Telephone Tips for Every Style

Telephone Tips for Every Style

Telephone Tips for the High-D Sales Professional

If you are a High-**D** sales professional, use this section to get better RESULTS!

Your biggest challenges with phone calls may be:

- Over confidence – you may ignore input from coaches, managers, and other sales people
- A desire to work alone- you may move out of the group area to be alone during a calling session
- Resisting the use of a script
- Coming across as too pushy or aggressive to prospective clients

Your desire to get results will serve you well. Remember to focus on relationships first and tasks second and you will achieve success. Your energy and focus will propel you to great heights when you balance your drive for results with sensitivity to people.

To enhance your calling success if you are a High-D:

- Stay open to coaching from people with a style different than yours.
- Stay with the team. You may learn something from someone else.
- Realize that the sales people who get the best results stick to a script.
- Use softer, less intense vocal tones. Remember that only 10% of the population is like you. That means that 90% of the people you call will not have your intensity.

Telephone Tips for the High-I Sales Professional

If you are a High-I sales professional, this section is ALL ABOUT YOU! Use this section to have more FUN!

Your biggest challenges with phone calls may be:

- Staying on task – you might get involved in conversations with other people in the room
- Keeping the phone calls short – you probably like to talk
- Organizing your call list – focusing to get everything on one sheet of paper prior to the call session could be a challenge
- Fighting the urge to mix personal calls with business calls

Once you get focused though, look out! You probably project great confidence and enthusiasm. You will naturally connect with many people because of your energy level. You need to pay attention to your prospective client's reaction. The same energy that helps you with many people could frustrate a High-**C** client. When you take the time to pay attention to the person on the other end of the phone, you should be able to adjust your style fairly easily. Most people enjoy talking with High-**I**'s.

To enhance your calling success if you are a High-I:

- Get organized before the call. Make sure your list is really a list (not a collection of note cards, business cards, and sticky pad notes). You will feel good about yourself if you can make lots of calls quickly and then get on to something even more fun!
- Reward yourself with something during the phone call session. For example, you could purchase a bag of your favorite candy and treat yourself to one piece after every 5 calls.

- Make sure your cell phone is charged and ready to go.
- Leave the small talk with co-workers for later.

Telephone Tips for the High-S Sales Professional

If you are a High-**S** sales professional, understanding this section will help you FEEL MORE COMFORTABLE with the **Sell Naked Sales System**.

Your biggest challenges with phone calls may be:

- Getting started – until you feel comfortable with how to make the calls, you may be hesitant. Outside observers may see this hesitancy as resistance.
- Feeling that you are bothering or interrupting the people you are calling. You may make excuses like, "It's almost lunch time, I don't want to bother them now" or, "It's early in the morning, I don't want to catch them just coming in the office." We know that this concern is very real for you because you tend to feel other people's concerns.
- Speaking too softly on the phone. While High-**D**'s might come on too strong, you might project a lack of confidence.
- Overcoming a fear of the unexpected. Concerns over wrong numbers, unexpected responses, or reaching someone other than who you intended to reach can all be swirling in your head at the same time.

If you have seen the movie, *Seabiscuit*, you can get a good mental picture of this style in action. Seabiscuit (the horse in the movie) started slowly and then came from behind to win. If you have High-**S** traits, you might perform like Seabiscuit – you may start slow and then finish strong. You may or may not currently be a star on the sales team, but you can become a star no matter where you start the process. Once you have a clear mental picture for HOW to get started, use your steady nature to keep going until you have done the job.

To enhance your calling success if you are a High-S:

- Distinguish between present doubts and past defeats. You may not believe in your ability to be successful at phone calling if you have had negative past experiences. Focusing on your past defeats feeds the fear that creates your present doubts. Everyone has some doubts. The structure of the **Sell Naked Sales System** will minimize the risk of repeating your past defeats or frustrations. Trust the process, and you can overcome your doubts.
- Raise your speaking volume and pace. You will sound more confident and friendly. Because you probably have a soft natural demeanor, you do not need to worry about sounding aggressive or pushy.
- Focus on how your product or service could help your prospective client. Remember – you are not bothering them with a sales call, you are calling to offer your help.
- Recognize that some people simply will not meet with you. When they reject your offer, they are not rejecting you.

Telephone Tips for the High-C Sales Professional

If you are a High-**C** sales professional, this section will give you the insights and understanding to assist you in your efforts to get greater VALUE from the time you invest in the sales process.

Your biggest challenges with phone calls may be:

- Over-analyzing every call and response. This over-analysis can lead to paralysis – not getting anything done. It might show up as critiquing yourself to an extreme. You have incredibly high standards; even small errors may seem like major failures to you.

- Thinking about the calls rather than doing them. Pushed to an extreme, your careful, plan-oriented nature can keep you from getting started. This issue can show up in a number of ways. If you think that you need to alphabetize your call list, re-organize your work area, or re-write your script before you place calls, this could be your challenge.
- Interacting with people on the phone. You may prefer working alone, so talking to someone on the phone could be out of your comfort zone. Your desire to deliver the perfect opening statement might cause you to hesitate... indefinitely.
- Sounding cold (emotionally) or boring to potential clients. If you are like many people with High-**C** traits, you may have a naturally consistent and calm voice (sometimes to the extreme of being monotone). Your potential clients could interpret this vocal tonality as lack of care or concern.

Once you overcome these challenges you can achieve great calling success. When you develop a script that you trust, your focused, intense desire for consistency will create results. Learn to deflect rejection by using your objectivity to separate your offer from your identity. When you do this, you can view rejection in a way that does not reflect on you or your performance. Your ability to plan and research can help you easily address any objections.

To enhance your calling success if you are a High-C:

- Separate individual call results from your identity. The **Sell Naked Sales System** increases the odds of success; it does not guarantee success on every call. Do not let any single response to your offer keep you from moving forward.
- Prepare in advance then get in motion and make the calls. Adjust to improve results after a rejection? Yes. Start at zero and re-plan your whole approach? No!

- Find a good opening line and use it. You do not need the perfect opening line.
- Smile when you are on the phone. Yes, we know that your prospective client cannot see you, but they can hear you. When you smile, your tone will change; and you will sound more warm and caring.

13

Make the CALL

Make the CALL

Now we have come to the time to put everything you have learned into action. It's time to make some phone calls. As you read this section and prepare to take action, remember what **CALL** represents:

- **C** CONNECT with the person on the phone
- **A** ANSWER the question, "Why are you calling me?"
- **L** LISTEN to their response
- **L** LOCK-IN the meeting

Phone Calling Sessions

If possible, we recommend that you schedule team calling sessions rather than working alone. In a group setting, you create more positive energy and enthusiasm. As a result, you book more meetings.

Tips to Improve Your Phone Calling Sessions:

- The first time you schedule a calling session, allow 3-4 hours. Once you get more comfortable with the script and have more practice addressing objections, you can work in 30-45 minute increments on a regularly scheduled basis.

- Schedule the calling session in a room large enough for each person to have a table. You do not want the calling session to sound like it originates from a telemarketing center. However, you get an electric synergy in a group setting. Make sure that people have plenty of room to work.

- Post a tracking chart that everyone can see. The tracking chart should have the following categories:
    - Number of calls
    - Number of appointments
    - Number of call backs
    - Number of "no's"
    - Number of morons

Note: We only use the word "moron" to lighten things up, not to label people. This category will be the smallest by far. You should reserve it for those calls involving truly rude or obnoxious people. These are the calls many sales people fear the most and will encounter the least. Keeping a record of these calls provides two benefits:

- It shows how rare these incidents actually are.
- It helps the group laugh it off to extinguish any negative effect the bad experience might have on the caller.

- Everyone present should have a **CALL** list with at least 50-75 names and numbers.
- Set a goal for the number of appointments the team will book. Create a team atmosphere.
- Everyone present should agree to:
    - Stay as close as possible to their script.
    - Stay in their seat until they make at least 10 calls (15 is even better).
    - Avoid lengthy conversations. Remember, you want to book appointments not chit-chat.
    - Have fun and support each other.

Key Thoughts to Remember While Calling for Appointments

- Your prospective client probably feels more motivated to eliminate a pain than to gain anything. For example, they will more likely act on getting rid of odors than they will on making a building smell fresh. During the call, listen for the words that reveal their displeasure or pain. Be ready to sell a solution to a problem rather than offer a product or a service.

- Always agree with your clients. When they give an objection or ask a question, agree with their perspective before you say anything else. Once you are in agreement about their concern or displeasure, recommend that they allow you to evaluate their problem more fully so that together you can find a solution.

- You are not really in a product fulfillment or service delivery business. You are actually in the pain elimination business. Find the pain they want to eliminate and then offer a solution to that.

Joe has a great story to illustrate this point:

I remember a sales person (I will call him Mike) who was new to sales and was nervously making cold calls. Mike stuttered and stammered through a very mediocre script. During his calls, he kept flipping back and forth in his notes and repeating himself. It was truly awful! So awful that everyone in the room stopped, listened and started laughing out loud. Surprisingly, he eventually managed to get an appointment. Everyone was amazed. I remember thinking "I guess you don't have to be good…You just have to do it!"

Here's the kicker. The prospective client on that call eventually became one of Mike's most loyal customers. They have maintained a great professional relationship for more than ELEVEN years as of the time of writing this story. They also became good friends.

One day, Mike mentioned that first, awful call to his friend and customer. To Mike's amazement, the customer said that he never thought the call was awful. In fact, he initially agreed to meet with Mike because he had a major frustration at the time. *He wanted to eliminate his pain, and Mike called with a solution to fill that specific need.*

What an epiphany! Prospective customers don't necessarily know or care how perfect the presentation or phone call is. They really only care about their own needs and their situation. This revelation freed Mike from much of his fear of the phone, and it became one of the most important sales lessons of his life. Find the need, fill the need, and CASH the CHECKS!

Gatekeeper - Friend or Foe?

Get to know the person who controls access to the decision-maker. We call this person the "gatekeeper." Your relationship with them is just as important as your relationship with the decision-maker. Work to develop a great connection with this person. Remember that the most important person you talk with during any given phone call is the one who answers the phone. Their impression of you will often determine whether you speak with anyone else or not.

This person cannot generally say yes to your proposal, but they can definitely say no. They might not use the word no, but their behaviors can. Maybe they will not let you speak with the decision-maker. They might continually defer your calls, and ask you to call back later. They could come across as rude and dismissive or sweet and friendly. Whatever they do, remember this idea:

Do everything you can to make the gatekeeper your friend.

People in a gatekeeper position normally feel responsible for protecting the decision-maker from unnecessary interruptions and pesky sales professionals. Generally speaking, they have an incentive to block you out. By letting you through the gate, they could receive consequences ranging from negative comments by the decision-maker to losing their job. In other words, *helping you get through to the decision-maker might cause discomfort for them.*

Always keep this thought in mind as you work with them. They may expect to receive more negative than positive consequences from helping you except in two special situations:

1. They really like you, or
2. You already have a strong connection with the decision-maker.

As a result, you only have two options when it comes to working with the gatekeeper:

1. Go out of your way to connect with them, or
2. Find a way to meet or contact the decision-maker that removes the gatekeeper from the process.

For our purposes, we will focus on the first approach – connecting with the gatekeeper. The second approach, while useful, lies outside the scope of this book.

To make the connection, remember these key facts about gatekeepers:

- They are people, too. They do not want to be used, manipulated, or persuaded to let you through. If they feel that you do not care about them, they will probably block you from the decision-maker.

- They usually work closely with the decision-maker. They generally understand the company's goals, challenges, and priorities. They have information that can help you. If you take the time to connect with them and develop mutual trust, you may learn some valuable information.

- They often have a trusted advisor relationship with the decision-maker. Treat them with the same respect you would the decision-maker.

- They are often part bloodhound. They can usually "smell a fake a mile off." When the gatekeeper asks the reason for your call, answer with the same basic script you would use for the decision-maker.

Keys to Successfully Working with the Gatekeeper:

- Ask for their name and use it during the conversation. Put it in your notes for future reference.

- Treat them with respect.

- Employ your knowledge of the **Model of Human Behavior** to make a friend.

- Use the script you have written for the decision-maker.
- Ask some of the probing questions you have planned for the decision-maker. Gatekeepers generally have the pulse of the organization. They can give you some great insights about the needs of the business. If they like and trust you, you might even gain what could be considered insider information.

Putting It All Together – A Quick Review

Since you created your script outline to follow the **CALL** method, you should have no problem following the flow of the phone call.

Now let's quickly summarize the process:

C **CONNECT** with the person on the phone

- Use the elevator speech from your script outline.
- Quickly work to build a connection based on how they answer the phone and ask questions.
  - Are they more outgoing or reserved? Listen for voice tone and pace when they answer the phone.
  - Match your tone and tempo to theirs.

A **ANSWER** the question, "Why are you calling me?"

- Use your script to guide you. Adjust your wording based on what you know about them at this point.
  - Are they more outgoing? Speak more quickly and with more volume.
  - Are they more reserved? Speak more slowly and with less volume.
  - Are they more task-oriented? Use thinking words.
  - Are they more people-oriented? Use feeling words.

  (Remember our tip on this point: If you have nothing that tells you otherwise, assume that they are people-oriented and use feeling words as your starting point.)

L **LISTEN** to their response

- Continue working to build a connection. Listen for clues that will help you schedule the meeting.
- Are they more task-oriented or people-oriented? Work the odds and start with a people or feeling oriented approach. You should adjust your approach based on their response to you.

L **LOCK-IN** the meeting

- Address any objections they offer and schedule the meeting, IF you sense that they qualify for your offer. Do not push hard on this point or shift into presentation mode. Remember that the purpose of the call is to make contact and to schedule an appointment. Your purpose is not to sell your product or service at this point in the relationship.
- Use your knowledge of the **Model of Human Behavior** to improve your odds.
  - Are they more of a **D** type? Be direct and focus on results.
  - Are they more of an **I** type? Use testimonials and stories. Let them know that you like them.
  - Are they more of an **S** type? Give them time to process. Slow down. Focus on help, support, and reducing stress/conflict.
  - Are they more of a **C** type? Answer their questions. Give them time to think and answer when you ask a question. Focus on quality, data, and excellence.

A Success Story

Do the pre-call preparations, group calling sessions, and the **CALL** method really work? Absolutely they do!

Joe has a story for us to demonstrate all of the elements of success in calling for appointments that we have already covered.

A large cleaning supply company contracted me to work with their sales professionals. The sales manager reported that the sales people worked so hard to service existing accounts that they would spend a great deal of time traveling around their territory picking up orders and not create new business. In his words, his sales people were *"order takers and not order makers."* The business had more capacity to help customers, but they had reached a plateau because of the sales people's reticence to contact potential new clients. The company had not grown in months.

First I worked with the sales team to build a solid understanding of the **Model of Human Behavior**. We discussed the different personality styles. Each person completed a personality profile assessment, and we discussed each person's strengths and blind spots. Before we began the calling sessions, they had a good foundation for success.

Next, I explained the **Sell Naked Sales System** calling process from start to finish. We completed all of the preparatory work. Then we scheduled a group calling session. In this calling session, I required the sales people to bring a call list of new potential

clients. I did not allow them to call old customers in an attempt to upsell. I wanted them to develop new business from this exercise.

The sales people came to the first calling session with different reactions: apprehension, mild anger, fear and a host of other negative emotions. They simply did not want to participate. I have seen this same reaction many times. In fact, it is the norm. As the coach, I had to set the right environment for each individual as they entered the room that day.

Knowing each sales person's personality style blend really helped me to help them with the calls. Taking my own advice, I met each person in a different way.

Dan (High-**D**) entered the room. I gave him a firm hand shake and said, "I know you know what you're doing. If you need anything, yell. Pick your spot and help me keep this outfit focused." (I spoke in short sentences. I showed that I respected him and had confidence in his abilities. I also asked him to help me control the group.)

When Susan (High-**S**) entered the room I grabbed both her hands and softly said, "We're going to have a great day. Susan, I'm going to help you all day. Where would you like to sit?" I then helped her get situated in a safe place. (Susan was out of her comfort zone and feeling insecure. I assured her I would help her, and I gave her a safe place to sit. I also held her hands. If your relationship is good, touch can often reassure a High-**S**. But, here's a word of caution: Do not touch a High-**C** unless you know them very well.)

As Charlie (High-**C**) entered – list typed, phone numbers ready – I said, "Charlie, that is an incredible list, let's get you organized in a good place so we can

start on time." (High-**C** types usually like organization and timeliness.)

Then, Irene (High-**I**) came in at the last minute. I greeted her with, "Hi, Irene. We're going to have fun today. Hey, is your cell phone charged?" (It wasn't.) I put her in a central location where she could be the center of attention. (Scolding Irene for a last minute arrival would make her look bad in front of other people. This would NOT increase her confidence. Irene remembering to bring her cell phone was positive. Charging it in advance would have been nice, but chastising her would not help. I just helped her find her charger and get the phone plugged-in. "Fun" is critical for High-**I**'s. So, I wanted her to know we would have fun. I seated her in the middle of the room because, High-**I**'s often like to know they will receive plenty of attention from everyone else.)

Once everyone was in place, we had a quick pre-call meeting. I shared the goals and guidelines. Each associate would make 50 calls. We would not get up the first time until each person made at least 10 calls. We would break for lunch. Then I said, "Hey team, I promise you will be glad we did this. This is going to increase your income and grow your company. You can do this, and I'm here to help. Relax and have fun. Let's go."

As the phone call session progressed, I walked around and listened. I made suggestions with statements like, "That was great, you might want to try this..." I did not correct anyone. I also helped them to remain focused on making calls by encouraging them to stay on the phone. Until people experience success, they will use almost any reason to stop

calling. I wanted them to stay in their seats, dialing their phones.

We kept the tracking chart current so that people could see their progress. Seeing progress really helps people stay motivated to keep going after they experience a rejection.

The group dynamics were great. People could see other people booking meetings. They even started to compete with each other. Everyone could see that the principles and techniques helped them to become successful.

In the first call session with this company, we had the following results:

- Sixteen (16) sales people present
- Made 400 phone calls
- Booked 74 meetings

In the second call session, they did even better:

- Nine (9) sales people present
- Made 300 phone calls
- Booked 71 meetings

All of the meetings we booked during these two sessions eventually happened. They had no cancellations or no-shows. About 80% of the meetings resulted in new sales.

Susan (our High-**S** sales person) achieved so much success that she received a promotion as a result of her improved results.

By applying the **Sell Naked Sales System**, this team truly became order makers.

Before we move on, let's look back at Joe's story to highlight a few key points:

- The sales team applied the calling principles and techniques we teach, and they drastically improved their success rate.
- Joe applied the same principles we recommend for working with client's in his work with the sales people. As a result, they listened to him and were willing to take his suggestions – exactly what you want to achieve with your clients.
- The sales team did not achieve 100% success. They did achieve greater success than they had previously experienced by staying active and allowing the process to work. After all, what value would most companies place on 145 meetings with ***new*** clients?
- Every sales person worked with a script and in an environment that best suited their style. Joe did not force a one-size-fits-all strategy on them. He taught them some basic principles and techniques, allowed them to personalize what they had learned, and then helped them apply the knowledge in the real world.

Joe's experience with the sales team in the story above shows the practical application of this sales system. We have now covered the foundational concepts. We have also described how to make the calls to get the meetings. In today's technology-driven world, a logical question is, "What if I get voice mail instead of a person?" We will address that question in our next chapter.

14

To Voice Mail…
or not to Voice Mail

(This applies to email too)

To Voice Mail...
or not to Voice Mail
(This applies to email too)

Our main focus in this book is helping you to understand both the principles and practices of effective telephone technique. Specifically, our concern is what to do once you have someone on the phone. We also recognize that in today's high-speed, information-overload business environment, you may have to work through voice mail and email to eventually speak with a decision-maker. While the main focus of our book is not voice mail or email techniques, we thought that we should share a few brief thoughts on the topic.

For many years we taught never, never, never leave a message. Then we found ourselves doing it out of necessity. Looking back, we realize that our reluctance to leave a message resulted from our inability to develop an effective way to do so. We had the same challenge with contacting people by email. Because we had so little success with voice mail and email, we taught people not to do either one.

After lots of trial and error, forced by the necessity to do something when we could not directly reach the decision-maker, we developed some insights into leaving messages that generally get a response.

Now we realize that most successful people appreciate persistence. You want your prospective clients to perceive you as persistent, but not pushy. So, now we say, yes, you should generally leave a voice mail message. Your messege should sound like your elevator speech. It should give your prospective client a reason to call you back.

Here are a few general guidelines for leaving messages:

- Decision-makers are busy people – you will probably have to leave more than one message.
- The larger the organization, the more messages you will probably have to leave.
- Keep it brief – Put yourself in the position of a business leader who has just arrived at their office to find twenty-five new voice mails, thirty-five new emails, and three people waiting to see them. Given this scenario, you probably only have 10 to 20 seconds to capture their attention.
- Avoid adding attachments to emails unless specifically requested by the client. The email message should not take more than 20 seconds to read.
- If you have a referral – use it. Use the name of the person who referred you early in the voice mail or put their name in the subject line of an email.
- Remember to lead with your client's need. Here are some examples:
  - Voice Mail – "This is ________________ from ____________ company. In reviewing your company's web site, I noticed that _________________ may be a concern you are facing. I have some **ideas** that will help _________________ . Let's talk. I believe it will be well worth your time. My number is _________________ . I'll give you a call tomorrow at _____ to see what will work best for both of us." (Notice the use of the word *ideas* in this message.)
  - Email – You have to get their attention with the subject line. For example: "Lowered employee turnover saves hospital $500,000 per year."

To illustrate the point, let's hear about one of Dawn's experiences:

> Recently, I wanted to contact an executive from a large national organization. I initiated contact by email with the following subject line:
>
> "I surveyed a few of your major clients."
>
> The text of the message simply read:
>
> "I talked to a few of your major clients and have developed some ideas that might increase your bottom line. We need to talk. What's better for you next Tuesday or Thursday?"
>
> I received a same day reply.

If you find that this issue continues to create challenges for you, we suggest that you look into resources specifically targeted towards email and voice mail technique. Hopefully, these brief tips will get you started in the right direction. In summary, leave messages and send emails. Just remember to make them brief and relevant.

15

The Success Mindset

The Success Mindset

> "If I had to select one quality, one personal characteristic that I regard as being most highly correlated with success, I would pick the trait of persistence. Determination. The will to endure to the end, to get knocked down seventy times and get up off the floor saying, 'Here goes number seventy-one.' "
>
> *- Richard M. DeVos*

Success in sales starts with your thinking, your mindset. It is not your actions, not your technique, and not your words; but rather your thoughts that lead to success. If you think like a successful person, you will eventually develop successful skills and techniques. These skills and techniques will contribute to your success, but they will not create your success. If you try to learn the skills without developing the right mindset, any success you achieve will be temporary.

With that thought in mind, we will share some attributes that contribute to what we like to call the "Success Mindset." We have found that these attributes work together to create lasting success.

Persistence

A survey of CEO's from Fortune 500 companies asked this question: "What is the most effective way for us to earn your business?" The number 1 response: BE PERSISTENT.

In the Introduction to this book, we cited our experience and the comments of a psychologist with regard to fear of the phone. We said that most people have at least some fear of the phone when used as a sales contacting tool. Since you have come to this point in the book, we can reasonably assume that you have experienced that fear for yourself.

We understand completely. We started there, but we overcame the fear. We overcame the fear with consistent and persistent action. We kept calling when we were afraid until we were no longer afraid. Along the way, we learned the thinking, skills, and approaches in this book.

"Constant exposure to dangers breeds contempt for them."

- *Marcus Aurelius*

From our experience and the shared experience of other people we have helped to improve their sales skills, we have learned this key point:

Stay in the game long enough and you will get results. Keep going and the fear goes away.

In other words, be persistent.

Joe has this to say about persistence:

Years ago I took a course in cardio-pulmonary resuscitation (CPR). One participant in the class asked this question: "How long do we continue to perform CPR on an unconscious person?"

This question has three simple answers:

- Until the person regains consciousness,
- Until medical professionals arrive, or
- Until rigor mortis sets in.

In sales, we call this level of persistence the CPR rule.

Simply put, the CPR rule says that sales people should continue to make contact until their prospective client changes their telephone number and/or begs to be left alone.

Look at these statistics that Herbert True, a marketing specialist at Notre Dame, found about the value of persistence in sales*:

- 60% of all sales come after 4 or more calls
- 44% of all salespeople quit trying after the first call
- 24% quit after the second call
- 14% quit after the third call
- 12% quit trying to sell their prospect after the fourth call
- Amazing! Only 6% of all sales people will make contact with a prospective client 5 or more times.

Since something like 60% of all sales happen after the fourth call, 82% of sales people are chasing 40% of all sales. This leaves 60% of all sales to the top 18% of sales people.

I have found that top sales people understand the CPR rule and apply it to their sales strategy.

*Quoted from "The Success Principles" by Jack Canfield

Dr. Rohm has one caveat to offer in regard to persistence based on his experience:

Over the years I have observed that there are three ways that most people deal with business clients. Some are effective and some are not. You choose which one you think is best.

1. Irritate

Constantly call your customers and send them emails weekly, or even daily. Flood their mailbox with brochures, advertisements and letters offering your product or service. Make yourself a first-class nuisance to them as often as possible. Call and interrupt them throughout the day.

I know you are thinking that nobody would do business that way. Yet, amazingly, I find that there are many companies and individuals who do that. They seem to think that if they "hound" their customers with the latest marketing techniques or all of their newest information, they will gain more business.

2. Ignore

Do not ever call your customers or get in touch with them. Do not take the time to contact them on any kind of regular basis. If they want to do business with you, they know how to find you. Always leave the ball in their court!

This is a strange approach as well, yet I have known many individuals who use it and then complain because they never have any business. When I ask

them about the last time they contacted their clients, they say, "Well, I was waiting for them to contact me. I figure if they want my services, they will call me."

3. In touch

Remember the story of *Goldilocks and the Three Bears?* The porridge Goldilocks liked was not too hot and not too cold, but just right. I have found this to be the approach that is "just right." In fact, this is the one we use at Personality Insights. We want to show persistence, and we want to avoid irritation.

We try to contact our clients every one to three months. We send them an email or give them a phone call just to let them know that we are thinking about them. We also tell them about the latest program, seminar or product that we have developed. We try to keep the contact brief, specific and to the point. Our purpose is to let our customers know that we have not forgotten them and that we would love to do business with them when the time is appropriate.

Using this approach, we have more business than we can really manage. It all goes back to this method of keeping in touch with our customers.

You might call it good customer service and that is partly true. But, it is more than that. It is letting the client know that we are thinking of them even if they do not have need of our services at the present time. It is planting seed that I have seen produce much fruit.

Let me offer one word of caution, though. The contact must be genuine. Many times our customer may not be interested in doing business with us at the time of our call. Yet, after the seed is planted,

sometimes in just a few days, they call to book a seminar or training program. We have made ourselves available by keeping in touch. It is a powerful tool that people respect and respond to with teamwork and cooperation.

Be persistent.

Patience

People with the Success Mindset also have patience. We do not mean complacence or a willingness to settle for the status quo. We do mean that they understand that true and lasting success takes time to build.

People with the Success Mindset know that their persistence will create results. So, they don't try to push any single client. They trust in the law of averages to eventually deliver results if they stay in the game. They can walk away from a prospective client when they realize that they don't really have what this client wants. They never force a sale.

As a result of their patience, they don't sacrifice long-term success for a short-term score. They act with integrity and honor towards all current and prospective clients so that they can maintain a lasting relationship with many clients.

Be patient.

Process

Because people with the Success Mindset recognize that selling follows a process, they work the process and not the client. This concept goes hand-in-hand with the idea of patience as part of the Success Mindset.

Sales people with this mindset know that they control the *number* of potential clients, and that their clients control the *pace* of the process.

They quit trying to push. Instead they find ways to stay in the process with their clients. They neither ignore, nor do they irritate. They initiate contact, get the process started, and then they relinquish control to their clients.

Work the process and not the client.

Production

Sales people with the Success Mindset have patience, and they trust the process. Having patience and trusting the process does not mean that they sit and wait for anyone. They invest their efforts where they can get the greatest return. They make many new contacts. They work at meeting and developing relationships with many new people. By creating more contacts, they create more potential opportunities. By creating more potential opportunities, they put themselves in a position to work the process rather than the client. (This activity focus helps them to have patience with each individual client.)

At the same time, they keep track of their results. They track their results so that they know what works for them and what doesn't. They maintain a clear focus on delivering new business and keeping good relationships with existing clients so that they have high production.

Produce results.

Partner

Remember our definition for selling? We said that selling is finding a way to help clients solve a problem or fill an unmet need.

In order to really apply this concept, we find that the ability and willingness to partner with other people is a large part of the Success Mindset. No one person can do everything well. Teams can succeed where individuals fail.

We have found that very few people achieve any lasting success on their own. Virtually every person who is successful in their own right also belongs to a support team. For example:

- Tiger Woods and his coaches
- Bud Abbot and Lou Costello
- Bing Crosby and Bob Hope
- Stan Laurel and Oliver Hardy
- Bill Gates and Paul Allen (Microsoft Corporation)
- Captain Meriwether Lewis and William Clark
- Sir Edmund Hillary and Tenzing Norgay (first to climb Mt. Everest)
- David Abercrombie and Ezra Fitch (Abercrombie & Fitch Clothiers)
- James Smith McDonnell and Donald Wills Douglas (McDonnell-Douglas Aircraft)
- William Proctor and James Gamble (Procter & Gamble)
- Richard Warren Sears and Alvah Curtis Roebuck (Sears Roebuck Company)
- Ben Cohen and Jerry Greenfield (Ben & Jerry's Ice Cream)
- Duncan Black and Alonzo Decker (Black & Decker Tools)
- Mark Victor Hansen and Jack Canfield (The Chicken Soup for the Soul series of books)
- John, Paul, George, and Ringo (The Beatles)
- Barry Gordy and Smokey Robinson (The Motown Sound)

We believe so strongly in this concept, you will notice that even the **Sell Naked Sales System** has a team of contributors. Everything any of us has ever done that you could call successful had some connection to other people in the making of that success.

Yes, every successful sales person must stand on their own. They have to make their own phone calls. They have to do their own presentations. They have to track their own results. But they will not achieve success if they cannot relate well with their office staff, or their production people, or their manager, etc. True success will come to people who understand and apply the power of partnering with other people.

Find trustworthy partners and build strong partnerships.

Prepare to Perform

Finally, the Success Mindset has an element of performance to it. People with the Success Mindset like to perform, are willing to perform, and are able to perform. They also know that thorough preparation comes before every good performance.

Like a musician or athlete, they understand the value of study and practice when they are not performing so that they can perform when necessary. This shows in their mindset because they have the discipline to read, study, practice, and prepare. They don't just wing it. To the outside observer, their performance might appear spontaneous. People with the Success Mindset recognize that what appears spontaneous in the moment actually comes from the effort to prepare in advance for the moment when the right phrase or comment makes the difference between getting the sale and losing it to someone else.

As we have heard it said, champions are made on the road and not in the ring.

Prepare for the performance.

So there you have it, the mindset, the principles, and the practices to successfully use the phone as a sales tool. We hope that what we have shared in this book will serve as a foundation for your success. Remember, though, that this book should represent part of your development as a sales professional and not all of it. Keep learning, growing, and practicing. Attend workshops and seminars. Read other books. Speak with mentors. Do everything you can to become a successful sales professional.

Now that you know what to do, you just need to go do it. Use what you have learned to book more meetings. We'll cover what to do to improve your odds of success once you're in the meeting in **Sell Naked In Person**, but don't wait to read that book before you get on the phone. Put yourself in a position to win. Knowing what to do and not doing it is no better than not knowing what to do. We look forward to hearing of your success as you strip away the barriers to your success and begin to…

… Sell Naked On The Phone.

"I ain't goin' down no more!"

- Rocky Balboa
from the movie "Rocky"

Appendix 1

The CALL Method

Book more meetings using the **CALL** method:

C **CONNECT** with the person on the phone

People will meet with you IF they like you or believe that you can help them solve a problem. Begin the phone call by connecting with your client. Learn skills to help you achieve a connection quickly.

A **ANSWER** the question, "Why are you calling me?"

Every person you call wants to know the answer to the question, "Why are you calling me?" Plan a good answer to this question and give it to them before they ask.

L **LISTEN** to their response

Learn to identify key information about your client simply by the way that they respond to your introduction on the phone.

L **LOCK-IN** the meeting

Use what you learned from listening to your client to phrase your offer to them in a way that shows them the value of meeting with you. Then lock-in the meeting.

Appendix 2

The Model of Human Behavior

Over twenty-four hundred years ago, keen observers of human nature began to notice predictable patterns of behavior. In time, these observations led to developing the **DISC Model of Human Behavior** to describe these patterns. Understanding these patterns in human behavior will help you improve your understanding of both yourself and others. The charts in this section illustrate the model and serve as a ready reference for you as you read this book.

Each person has an internal motor that drives them. This motor is either fast-paced, which makes some people more **OUTGOING**. Or, it is slower-paced, which makes other people more **RESERVED**. The illustration to the right shows this difference graphically. The shading of the arrows from lighter to darker indicates varying intensities of these drives. Close to the midline shows less intensity in the motor activity, therefore light shading. Towards the outer edge shows more intensity in the motor activity, therefore darker shading. You may be extremely **OUTGOING** or extremely **RESERVED**. Or, you may be only moderately **OUTGOING** or moderately **RESERVED**.

Just as each person has a motor which drives them, everyone also has an internal compass that draws them towards either Tasks or People. Some people are more **TASK-ORIENTED** - drawn towards tasks. Other people are more **PEOPLE-ORIENTED** - drawn towards people. The illustration to the left shows this difference graphically. The shading of the arrows from lighter to darker indicates varying intensities of this compass drive. Close to the midline shows less intensity in this compass drive, therefore light shading. Towards the outer edge shows more intensity in this compass drive, therefore darker shading. You may be extremely **TASK-ORIENTED** or extremely **PEOPLE-ORIENTED**. Or, you may be only moderately **TASK-ORIENTED** or moderately **PEOPLE-ORIENTED**.

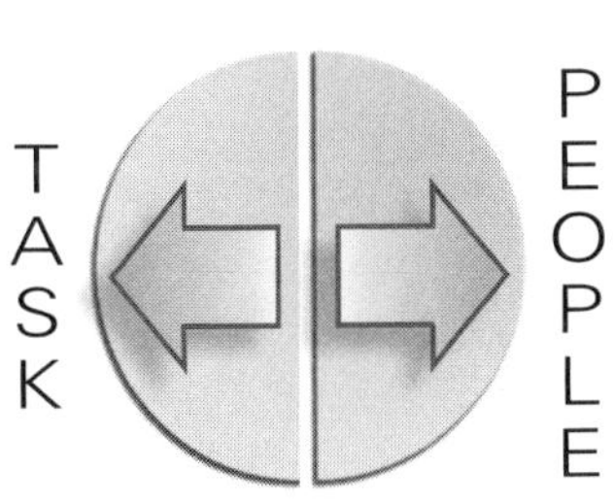

When you put together both the Motor and Compass Activity drawings, you see the **Model of Human Behavior** illustrated on the **next page**.

In the diagram on the next page, notice that each DISC type has a group of descriptive words that relate to behavioral characteristics of that personality style. These descriptive words show traits or tendencies that describe each type. The main characteristic trait for each type is used as the representative word for that type: Dominant, Inspiring, Supportive, and Cautious.

Notice that people who are:

Outgoing and Task-oriented are...	DOMINANT
Outgoing and People-oriented are...	INSPIRING
Reserved and People-oriented are...	SUPPORTIVE
Reserved and Task-oriented are...	CAUTIOUS

Here are some shortcuts you can use in discussing the different types of people:

the	DOMINANT	type is also known as High-D
the	INSPIRING	type is also known as High-I
the	SUPPORTIVE	type is also known as High-S
the	CAUTIOUS	type is also known as High-C

This model can help you understand people by describing four main, or primary, personality styles. However, *each individual person will display some of all four personality styles*. This blend of styles within each person is called a style blend. Each person's style blend will have more of some traits and less of others. The types that are strongest in a style blend are called High-Styles. The types that are less prevalent in a style blend are called Low-Styles.

Outgoing – Task-Oriented	**Outgoing – People-Oriented**
Dominant **D**irect **D**emanding **D**ecisive **D**etermined **D**oer	**I**nspiring **I**nfluencing **I**mpressionable **I**nterested in people **I**nteractive **I**mpressive
Percentage of population: 10–15%	Percentage of population: 25–30%
 **D**	**I**
C	**S**
Percentage of population: 20–25%	Percentage of population: 30–35%
Cautious **C**alculating **C**ompetent **C**onscientious **C**ontemplative **C**areful	**S**upportive **S**table **S**teady **S**weet **S**tatus Quo **S**hy
Reserved – Task-Oriented	**Reserved – People-Oriented**

Personality Style Blends

Only a very small percentage of people have a personality style blend that is just one High-**DISC** type. Most people (about 80%) have two High-**DISC** types and two Low-**DISC** types in their style blend. This means that one **DISC** type may be highest in your style blend, but you probably also have a secondary **DISC** type which is also high. This secondary type supports and influences the predominant type in your style blend. For example:

> A person who has the **I** type highest and **S** as a secondary high type, would be an **I/S** style blend.
>
> A person who has the **I** type highest and **D** as a secondary high type, would be an **I/D** style blend.

While both of the people in the example above are High-**I** types, the difference in their secondary traits would make them very different people.

It is less common, but not highly unusual, to have a third high type in a style blend (i.e. **I/SC** or **I/SD**). Approximately 15% of people have three High-**DISC** types and one Low-**DISC** type in their style blend.

This blending of personality styles in each person helps to account for the large variability among people even though there are only four primary types described by this model.

As you looked at the style descriptive words for each type, you may have felt that you could relate to some of the words in several, or even all, of the **DISC** types. The styles where most of the words describe you are probably your High-Styles. The styles where only one or two words describe you are probably your Low-Styles. That is okay. This is just a reflection of your unique style blend.

Personality Combinations

When two people interact, their style blends come together to form a combination. This combination is unique to each interaction of people. Adding a third person to the mix forms a different combination. The real power in understanding personality information lies in developing the ability to recognize these different combinations and to adapt yourself to each new situation.

Applying What You Have Learned

If we can understand each other and adapt to each other better, we can enjoy one another more and increase our productivity at the same time. Dr. Rohm's book, *Who Do You Think You Are... anyway?*, explains many of the factors which work for and against harmony in all kinds of relationships. In the **Sell Naked Sales System**, we specifically explore how the combination of your style, along with the style(s) of your customers, affects the sales process. We also offer tips on how to make your presentations more convincing based on the style(s) of your customers.

The great news is that you can learn to relate better to virtually everyone! Your ability to understand and apply personality information to build stronger relationships is known as your Personality Quotient (PQ). Learning experts say that people can do little to change their Intelligence Quotient (IQ). They say that IQ is fairly fixed at birth. However, unlike your IQ, you can develop your PQ. That allows you to have greater success with anyone you meet, whatever their style.

The **Sell Naked Sales System** will help you move through the four steps to raising your PQ so that you can achieve greater success as a Sales professional.

We compare the process of raising your **PQ** to taking a trip. On a trip you have four things:

1. A map
2. A starting point
3. A destination, and
4. A route.

When you work with other people, you have four similar steps:

Learn the PATTERN – The DISC **Model of Human Behavior** is your "map" on this journey of working with other people. Use it to describe your observations about people and their behaviors.

Make it PERSONAL – identify your "starting point" by applying the pattern to describe your PERSONAL perspective.

Apply the "map" to other PEOPLE – Specify your "destination" by using the pattern to understand other PEOPLE.

Use your observations in a PRACTICAL APPLICATION – Plan the "route" you will use. Employ the pattern for greater success by planning and adapting your approach for each client and each situation.

So, you have four steps to raising your **PQ**:

Learn the Pattern
Make it Personal
Apply it to other People
Use it in Practical Applications

With the **Sell Naked Sales System**, you apply the **Model of Human Behavior** to sales. You can also apply the Model to a wide range of other applications:

- Leadership
- Communication
- Team building
- Parenting
- Time Management

Additional suggested reading on the **Model of Human Behavior** (by Dr. Robert A. Rohm):

- *You've Got Style*
- *Who Do You Think You Are...anyway?*
- *Positive Personality Profiles*

Resource Materials

You've Got Style

Dr. Robert A. Rohm

This book is a great guide on understanding yourself and others. It gives all the foundational information about the four personality styles, and it also includes chapters on adapting your style and building better teams. Simple enough to understand, practical enough to apply!

Presenting with Style

Dr. Robert A. Rohm and Tony Jeary

A collaborated effort between Tony Jeary (*Mr. Presentation*) and Dr. Robert Rohm (*World Class Communicator*) this book is a must for those who do presentations of any kind whether that is sales or public speaking.

How I Raised Myself from Failure to Success in Selling

Frank Bettger

(Foreword by Dr. Robert A. Rohm)

A business classic, *How I Raised Myself from Failure to Success in Selling* is a must read for anyone whose job it is to sell. Whether you are selling houses or mutual funds, advertisements or ideas – or anything else – this book is for you. No matter what you sell, you will be more efficient and profitable – and more valuable to your organization – when you apply the author's keen insights.

Personality INSIGHTS PRESS

For more information go to: www.personalityinsights.com

The Discovery Report is over 52 pages. You create your personal Discovery Report by completing an online Personality Assessment. The report includes specific instructions to help you achieve personal success. This report will propel you to a new level of achievement. It highlights your individual strengths, the value you bring to an organization, and ways to maximize your gifts and abilities on a team. This positive, encouraging, and comprehensive report focuses on: 1) helping you build better relationships, and 2) targeting your abilities to produce maximum results.

With this report, you will discover STRENGTHS and STRATEGIES to help you understand the needs of others. This understanding helps you ACHIEVE better bottom-line results — both personally and professionally. This practical, principle-driven guide provides useful tips on how to improve performance in your business. With this information, you will improve your personal productivity, communication, and teamwork skills.

For more information go to:
www.discoveryreport.com
or
www.personalityinsights.com

Coming soon...

Sell Naked in Person

THE BOOK

Stripping Away the Barriers to Your Success in Sales

To learn more about personality styles and to get

Four Free Online Lessons,

please go to:

www.personalityinsights.com

On the home page click on the Red Free Offer icon

Take the 4-part online course

Life is all about relationships. Our ability to achieve success in life is directly linked to our ability to get along with others. What if it were possible to literally change the way you relate to everyone in your life? NOW IT IS! Take a few minutes to work through a **FREE** interactive, online four part mini-series called Better Relationships by going to www.personalityinsights.com. Just click on the red button that says "**FREE OFFER**." You will be amazed at the insight you will gain into yourself and others!

We hope you enjoy the lessons!

To learn more about your personality go to

www.discoveryreport.com

and click in the icon:

Personality

Lab!

Experiment. Learn. Grow.

What is your unique personality blend? Did you know that you have a mixture of 4 major traits in your personality?

Try this short quiz to get an estimate of your strongest traits. Please note that this is **NOT** our full personality assessment - this is just a quiz. This quiz is only intended to estimate traits which may be prevalent in your personality style. We invite you to "***experiment***" with this **free tool** to get an idea about your personality style.

TM
Personality
INSIGHTS
PRESS